ALL MEN ARE SIMPS; THE SIMP CHRONICLES, VOL 1

By Dita Leventhal

This book is lovingly dedicated to my children, whose presence infuses every endeavor with purpose and meaning.

I extend my heartfelt gratitude to E.L. for their unwavering support, urging me to see this project through and pursue my aspirations.

To A.M., I am profoundly grateful for recognizing my potential and steadfastly believing in me.

And to T.G., my guiding force, whose tenacity and encouragement propelled me forward even in moments of doubt.

This dedication is also for all the resilient girls out there who have faced shame, ridicule, and negging. Your perseverance is an inspiration, and I fervently believe that you are destined to manifest the life of your dreams.

CONTENTS

INTRODUCTION

All men are simps. This truth is as clear as day. Every XY chromosome carrier is a simp, without exception. In the realm of simpdom, there is no hierarchy; all are equally simp. Even the most powerful and high-ranking man carries the simping gene, encoded deep within his DNA.

This fact has been successfully hidden from the masses, creating misery and confusion. The failure to properly harness simpdom has given birth to a battle of the sexes that has ensured that neither women nor men or happy but are unable to articulate why.

We exist in an era where the average American/Western woman has been psychologically manipulated into taking the lead like men while men have been manipulated into receiving like women. This has extinguished the polarity that forged mutually beneficial unions. American women have forgotten how to tap into their innate ability to inspire simping in men. Men have forgotten that simping makes them happy and fulfilled.

We have penned this book to rekindle women's awareness to the power they wield. This knowledge was not passed down to contemporary women from their mothers, who were preoccupied with unshackling themselves from the toxic aspects of patriarchy and inadvertently let slip valuable secrets of extracting simping.

Instead, these secrets have been rediscovered from an unexpected source: women from developing countries, desperate to escape their circumstances, reinvented the art of the finesse. These third world brides have mastered the skill of obtaining whatever they desire from Western men, who often refused to provide these basics to their own women back home!

On the surface, this book is tailored for women living in foreign countries who aspire to emigrate to Western countries through courtship and marriage as demonstrated by the women who have successfully achieved it.

However, its scope extends much deeper. This handbook is a guide to eliciting simp behavior from men, offering principles that women everywhere can benefit from.

We invite any women intrigued by this book to delve deeper and explore the art of the Finesse. Here, you will discover how to leverage your power as a woman to your advantage.

****This book is for entertainment purposes only****

CHAPTER ONE

THE PERFECT MOMENT

We are poised in a unique moment in time. A convergence of factors leaves a wide-open opportunity for foreign women to capitalize on the romantic void created by:

1. Feminism/women's liberation
2. Red pill philosophy
3. Level-Up movement

And made easier by

4. Affordability and ease of international travel.
5. Worldwide communication via social media
6. English as the business language of the world

We will do a deep dive into all these elements and how to exploit them to realize our ambitions.

The fact is, thanks to technology, western men are readily accessible to prospective brides, even in more rural/remote areas of the world. This makes the objective of marriage and living in the USA/ Canada/Europe/Australia/New Zealand easier than ever.

Moreover, this book is written to dissect and dismantle the contradictory web of advice propagated by male influencers on how to properly secure a husband. We, the TWG (Truly Wonderful Girls), approach this advice with a critical perspective and constantly remind ourselves that when setting our bait to attract the right partner-- DON'T ASK THE FISH.

Now that we have given you a brief overview, let's get into your motivations for embarking on this lifestyle.

   Note: This book is for entertainment purposes only. Enjoy!

CHAPTER TWO

WHAT IS YOUR WHY

The women reading this book are living in disparate parts of the world: the Philippines, the Ukraine, Colombia, and so on.

Some of us are educated, others did not have the luxury of going to school.

Often, we had older sisters, aunts and mothers who married their primary school sweethearts.

They married for love. They married for the tingle they felt when they first met.

After the ceremony, they quickly learned that love doesn't pay the bills.

We watched them struggle to keep a roof over their heads, put food on the table, and clothes on their backs.

Alternatively, your circumstances may not have been as dire. Your family had a fairly decent home, but they lacked the means for anything beyond the essentials.

You looked on with longing as the rich kids were chauffeured to ballet lessons and went on vacations to Europe.

They would return and frolic beside their inground swimming pool with GI Joes, Barbies, and Lego sets while you, the daughter of the housekeeper, played house with corn husks.

You blinked from the glare of the 3 carat diamond earrings worn by the housewives as they played tennis, indulged in massages and spa treatments and socializing at the country club.

Now, you are an adult. You turned 18. Soon, many of your school chums opt to marry boys from the village. Of those, most quickly become pregnant and bear multiple children--perpetuating the cycle of poverty or subsistence.

You have several options.

Option A:

At best, your husband is a civil servant in the city, earning enough to provide meals at home, but not for dining out more than once a month. A vacation may happen once or twice in a lifetime after saving frugally. He is intelligent, but not particularly ambitious, lacking the network, pedigree and charisma to advance beyond his station in life. He is a toady to his superiors at work, but desires to be the leader at home, while expecting you to work (in and out of the house) to ease his burden.

Option B:

At worst, you marry an uneducated laborer. Statistics show that uneducated men have the highest propensity for domestic violence and addiction. The adorable, dimple cheeked boy with whom you fell madly in love in primary school has developed a gut from drinking beer and leathery skin from toiling outdoors in the sun. When he comes home from work he is physically and mentally exhausted. He has checked out of contributing to the running of the household; that is woman's work. He is full of rage for his menial station in life...and who bears the brunt of his frustration? His wife and children, of course. You will receive no sympathy from law enforcement when he backhands you, or worse. Abusing women is not viewed as a crime in your country--it is part and parcel of being married.

But these are not the only options, surely. Why not seek a well-off man from my country of origin?

Option C:

Unlike the United States, our countries are not melting pots. The blend of cultures cemented into social strata that is highly resistant to upward mobility. Wealthy families tend to marry members of other wealthy families. You may be the exception yes; but to accomplish this you must put yourself in the vicinity of these prospects and work twice as hard to satisfy the gatekeepers. Often, you must be an outlier in terms of beauty, educational achievement, or fame, to penetrate these circles. It is not impossible, but it will take a lot of fortitude and thick skin to brave the hoops you must jump through and the family disapproval you must endure to survive the marriage...if you even reach that rung. "Patrician" men from developing countries often spend their youth entertaining lovely ladies with whom they go to work and school, only to settle down with their "own kind."

But what if you were not valedictorian of your high school? What if you are cute but not tall or beautiful enough to walk the catwalks of Milan?

What if you didn't have access to this book and you married and divorced Option A or B or were ghosted by Option C? What if Option A,B, or C left you with children before their exit?

Never fear. All is not lost. No matter how remote your village, or how isolated your town is—if you have access to the internet, you have options.

CHAPTER THREE

CHOOSE YOUR OWN ADVENTURE

Option D:

You are now 23 years old. Or you are 35 years old. Or you are 50.

You have seen what your sisters have gone through, struggling financially, or you have experienced it yourself.

In the evenings, after a smog filled bus commute from working in the fields or the factories or the office, you return to a messy home.

Your husband is either out drinking with his buddies or watching soccer on the television. You are greeted by neither a kiss nor a hug, nor questioned about how your day went. He nods and grunts hello, not looking in your direction.

If you are unmarried, your parents verbally assault you with a list of never-ending chores and an admonition of what will happen to you if you die an old maid, unmarried and alone.

If married, your children run and hug your legs, telling you about their day, wishing you could be home with them.

Your toothless mother, her eyes surrounded by deep set lines, wipes her hands on her apron, and smiles widely despite the hard life that has broken her body and her spirit.

You sigh and change the channel on the 15-year-old television. A "Friends" rerun is broadcast on the grainy screen. Your eyes dart from Joey and Chandler's apartment in Greenwich Village to your threadbare couch and broken lamp, tied together by twine.

You wonder, for a split second, and think, *if only.* If only I lived in

America. Where the streets are paved with gold. Where I could reinvent myself. If only I had a chance to escape this provincial life. Why is it that some women are blessed with the luck to be born in the greatest country on earth? While your life feels so unfair?

Your phone dings. You look at the text. It is your cousin, telling you that Dita is getting married and moving to America?

"Dita?" you exclaim. "But Dita is 10 years older, is divorced and has a teenage son! Who is she marrying?"

"An American", your cousin whispers. "He's old and ugly, though. He looks like Kentucky Fried Chicken."

"You mean Colonel Sanders?"

"Yes him. He is bringing her and Jaden to America!"

You listen slack jawed as your cousin spills the tea on Dita's groom.

You personally have not had much contact with Dita. She has always been a bit of a nonconformist. She moved to the capital after high school in hopes of advancing her singing career. Although she never made it to the big leagues she did make a living for herself singing at lounges and clubs. She supposedly had a brief marriage that resulted in her son's birth, although there was doubt about his legitimacy.

Curious, you call Dita. Dita tells you about her whirlwind courtship with Larry, an American who owns a construction company in Chicago.

They met 6 months prior online. Two weeks after messaging, he flew to the capital. Sparks flew; she was just as lovely in person as she was over the phone. They were inseparable for a month as she gave him a tour of their country. He respectfully behaved as a gentleman. Four months later Larry decided he didn't want to spend another day apart from his beloved. He proposed and Dita accepted.

Dita texts photos of the 4-bedroom home he owns with a pool in the back yard. *Just like the one I dreamed of,* you think.

Dita and Jaden were packing up to leave on a weekend flight to the US, paid for 100% by Larry.

"Oh my gosh, Dita," you say breathlessly. "I wish I were in your shoes."

"I'm not that special," Dita laughs, self-aware of her

circumstances. "I'm not the prettiest or the youngest or the smartest. But I am the most resourceful."

"Some people are lucky, I guess," you say mournfully, looking at the secondhand furniture shabbily decorating your humid, non-airconditioned house. A dusty fan whirs as flies decide where to land.

"It's not luck," Dita says. "It's intention. What is your intention for your life?"

"I dunno. To be happy, I guess. Healthy?" You are stumped.

"No. Be honest for once. Women, we are conditioned to lie to ourselves. We are ashamed to say what we want. What do you want? A nice house? A new car? To be away from your parents?"

"Yes! I want all of that! I want...money. Enough money to buy nice things. For my children. To send them to good schools. To put them in all the activities they want...to go to America."

Dita says the magic words:

You that you have the power to manifest anything you desire. It's in your hands.

"I wish I had your faith, Dita," You say.

"I meant literally," Dita says. "The phone in your hands. It is a genie's lamp."

CHAPTER FOUR
YOUR CHOICE

Where there is a will, there is a way. She recounts the trajectory that landed her in the promised land.

After Dita's husband left, she was forced to find a means to support herself and her son. Desperate, she found a housekeeping job at a hotel in the financial district.

There, she observed the habits of the businessmen who frequented the lobbies and lounges of the upscale hotel.

Most were alone. They would sit in the bars with other foreigners and complain about their lives back home. The divorced men complained about their ex-wives "divorce-raping" them and taking them for everything they owned (These men equated the equitable division of their assets as looting their hard-earned money and property, even if their spouses worked and contributed to the household income). Their children, if they had any, despised them and blamed them for the failed marriage.

Some of the men were younger, socially awkward and quiet. They could be categorized as "incels" (involuntary celibate men), men who were so physically and emotionally distasteful that they were rejected as romantic partners. Though they were approaching 30, many confessed to having never kissed a girl, let alone be involved in a relationship.

Why had their marriages failed? Why were these young men sexless and alone?

It was not the hours they spent scrolling on their phones; nor was it their inability to plan dates and romance. It could not possibly be the amount of time they spent playing video games, watching porn, nor their lack of help around the house or the children. Not the wandering eye, or the secret Tinder account. Impossible!

Dita noticed that these men accepted zero responsibility for the demise of their marriages or lack of dating success.

The mastermind of men at the bar came to a brilliant conclusion. It was the women's fault!

They determined that feminism ruined women's brains, and that it rendered them incapable of love, pair bonding, and loyalty. Physically, western women were obese and unattractive, yet felt entitled to the fidelity of "Chads". Chads were defined as Alpha Men: over 6 feet tall, earning 6 figures, and with a 6 carat ring in their pocket poised for a proper proposal.

The only solution was to avoid women altogether and join MGTOW (Men going their own way). The found fulfillment in other ways: by stacking cash, and fishing or golfing with their bros. Being alone had to be better than being nagged by an ungrateful and temporary partner who would be chomping at the bit to monkey branch to the next guy the minute he didn't kowtow to her edicts. "She's not yours, it's just your turn," was one of their favorite aphorisms.

They shared a hearty chuckle over the notion, but upon deeper reflection, they devised a more viable plan. After all, their deepest fear was the specter of loneliness, and the thought of living out the rest of their lives without intimacy was equally daunting. The prospect of dying alone and sexless was terrifying.

Was there a more promising path than complete celibacy? The lads glanced at the local talent serving them food, fluffing their pillows, and organizing their schedules. Instead of resorting to isolation or self-pleasure, why not pursue foreign babes? Why foreign women, you might wonder? It's because feminism had yet to reach their homelands, leaving them untouched by the influence of equal rights propaganda and girl-boss attitudes. The men believed that foreign women embodied qualities such as submissiveness, compliance, and soft femininity.

Even more appealing, foreign women were often not overweight, a contrast to American women who, they claimed, often neglected their health. This assertion conveniently overlooked the fact that these men struggled with beer bellies and balding heads of their own.

They clinked their beer bottles in a toast to better times, and better women, ahead.

Dita listened with rapt attention and diligently took notes about the "red pill" concepts. She delved into their beliefs on the online platforms where they congregated and bemoaned the state of western women. The fickle whims of women, she learned, were seen as the beginning of the decline of civilization. Their refusal to maintain a thin and attractive appearance, and to behave in a submissive and respectful manner, while expecting unrestricted access to men's wallets, was deemed outrageous. Someone had to hold women accountable, and the online alpha males were eager to take on this task.

The next time Dita received her paycheck, she signed up for an international dating website and uploaded smiling photos that highlighted her physique. In her bio, she described herself as a fit, feminine and traditional woman who relished cooking for and caring for masculine men of any age , emphasizing that she does not discriminate based on age.

"That's how you met Larry," you interject.

Not precisely, Dita says. She uploaded her profile on several dating sites and practiced rotational dating.

"Rotational dating?" you ask.

"Talking to several men at once," Dita quips. "May the best man win!"

You gasp. All of the women you know date one man at a time. How did Dita manage all these men?

"It takes practice. I made mistakes along the way. But I learned." Dita confessed that she fumbled the bag before she figured out the exact formula for landing what she called a "whale".

"I will teach you how to fish," Dita says with a sly wink. "Are you willing to learn?

"But Dita," you say, blushing. "How about applying for a visa? Maybe a job with sponsorship? Surely there must be another way to get to America besides marriage."

"There is," Dita replies. "It might take years to get a work visa. Do you have years to wait?"

No. You do not. You've wasted enough of your years. You catch a glimpse of yourself in the mirror and see the lines forming around your eyes. A preview of your mother's face, from long hours bent over, harvesting crops outdoors in the sun. Your hands are not quite as rough as hers. Yet.

"I don't know about you, but I like the path of least resistance. I like to get from point A to point B in the quickest way possible."

You slowly nod yes. "I'm ready."

"Wise choice. Let's begin with your education," Dita says.

CHAPTER FIVE

LONELY MEN

There is a loneliness epidemic among men in the US, Canada, Australia, New Zealand, and across the Western world.

This loneliness is shameful to men as it contradicts the image they have of themselves.

They see themselves as ruggedly individualistic, freedom loving lads who find fulfillment by conquering the world (and women) alongside their cadre of bros while achieving their goals. They believe that the adoration and companionship of women are secondary to, but not essential for, their worldly pursuits—or so they claim.

In fact, many men view themselves as lone wolves who could happily spend their lives as bachelors, as long as their material, physical and leisure needs are met.

However, we, as women, intuitively know that this is a lie. Men often deceive themselves. They like being lied to! These lies soothe their ego and provide a dose of "copium" to numb the deep crisis that lies at the core of the male condition.

A wife gives a man meaning. She gives him something to strive for and serves as a muse for him to channel his untapped talents into creating abundance. Throughout history every great man had a muse, who was a substrate for his greatness, from Leo Tolstoy to Coretta Scott King. Women are often inaccurately labeled as "chaos," when in reality, they are the stabilizing force in a man's life.

Statistics show that 60% of men consider their wives to be their best friends, as opposed to 27% of wives who consider their husbands to be their best friend. This highlights the fact that husbands rely heavily on their wives for their social and emotional needs.

Males are extremely vulnerable to the widowhood effect. In the year after losing a spouse, men are 70% more likely to die within a year than men who didn't lose a spouse. Loneliness literally kills men!

It is no wonder 70% (85% in Europe) of dating app users in the US are men, a lopsided ratio that illustrates man's hunger for companionship.

CHAPTER SIX

THE TRUTH

This is a truth that Men may never concede to, but that we as women, must harness and use to our advantage.

Men are lonely. Their greatest fear is not that they will be destitute. Or be without friends. Their greatest fear is being alone, of dying alone. Of being unloved.

It is a truth that has been known for thousands of years.

In the divinely inspired word of Bible, the Lord created Eve for Adam because "It is not good for man to be alone." The Lord put Adam to sleep and created Eve from his rib, so that when he woke up, he would have a companion. Because Eve was created from his body, Man was doomed to feel incomplete without a woman in his life.

Women give life meaning. They create life and they make men feel alive.

As a child, he was loved unconditionally by his mother, who clothed, fed, cleaned and cooked for him. He did nothing to earn it, he received it simply by existing. As her son of her flesh he was the center of her universe.

As he grew into an adult, he discovered that the rest of the female population did not find him adorable nor did they cater to him the same way his mother did.

He learned that in order earn a woman's love, he needed to work for it—through courtship, acts of service, and provision. However, he would also learn that he could never really possess a woman's love, as she had the ability to withdraw it at any time if her needs were not met.

This realization led to a deep resentment for many men who termed this as a "burden of performance". It felt unfair that to be respected as a man in his home, in his bed and in the world at large, that he needed to constantly prove his competence.

A woman, by contrast, need only "be", not "become". From a man's point of view, women have it easy. Whether she works, is a housewife, or an education is irrelevant, because nothing is expected of her. She will be protected and provided for, whether it is by her father, the government, or her husband.

Leaving their mother's skirts, men long to feel the love, attention and care they enjoyed as babies, and unconsciously seek to recreate it in adulthood. Men want to feel like they are loved for "themselves" and not for what they can provide. They yearn for a love like their mother's unconditional love, who will also cook, clean, and give them monkey sex.

The irony is that, when a man is in LOVE, he will want to provide. He will want to give you gifts. He will want to pay your bills. He will buy your plane ticket. He will sponsor your visa. He will love your children, even if he is not their biological father.

So much of a man's existence revolves around procuring a woman's attention and admiration. He will work hard, earn money, drive luxury cars, pick up interesting hobbies, all to impress women in the hopes that her rays of sunshine will evaporate the loneliness that follows him like a shadow.

As women, it is our job to exploit this desire and finesse it to our advantage.

The next section will outline what men consider to be the root cause of their contemporary state of loneliness: feminism and women's rights. It is important not to skip it so that you understand the reasons why men seek foreign wives in the first place. This will help you understand how to leverage their belief that western women are spoiled, entitled princesses ruined by "equal rights"- in your favor.

Never suspecting that by properly harnessing this knowledge, you will be transformed into a spoiled, entitled princess who will enjoy the same privileges as your American sisters in the greatest nation on Earth.

Better yet: He will think it was his idea!

CHAPTER SEVEN

RETVRN

In the good old days, men were men and women knew their place. They married young. Men worked, took care of their wives and children. Women were grateful for their husbands. Divorce rates were low.

If only we could "RETVRN", the twitter manosphere bemoans, life would be perfect. As proof of how far a mighty empire has fallen, they post videos of women skipping church to twerk at the club well into the night—and well into their thirties.

According to bro science, all women, even the hot ones, will eventually hit "the wall"—a line of demarcation that begins when a woman turns 25. They are comforted by the belief that a woman's comeuppance is ushered in by the appearance of "the wall" – the crossroads in a woman's lifespan when her beauty (her superpower) fades. With each successive year, as she grows older, her sex appeal and fertility declines (and thus her value), until she becomes invisible to men.

They believe that a woman's youth is spent effortlessly receiving Chad's attention, while ignoring the "good guys". When she hits the wall and is "ran through", she no longer can compete for Chad's attention and she has to settle for a "beta cuck" who will provide for her despite her high body count (number of sexual partners).

The sex and affection starved beta cuck will be grateful for his 30-year-old bride, even though her ride on the "cock carousel" (the hundreds of men she has slept with) has ruined her ability to pair bond and she could never properly love her husband let alone her children.

Despite her promiscuous history, her standards will be exceptionally high. She will demand nothing less than a man who stands at least 6 feet tall, earns a six-figure income, and presents a ring with at least 6 carats. If a man falls short of this extensive checklist, she will either reject him outright or, if she condescends to give him a chance, she will harbor resentment for his perceived inadequacy. If she is an expired "egg carton", the beta cuck is her last remaining option.

A woman is incapable of love. She only loves what a man can provide her. She can revoke her affections any time he refuses her unreasonable demands.

Sounds ridiculous, doesn't it? First of all, the data clearly shows that a high body count adversely affects both women and men about equally (a 4% difference between the sexes). Statistically, only a small percentage of people engage in promiscuous behavior to begin with—they are termed the "promiscuous 10 percenters". The 10 percenters swap partners among their own in unstable situationships, while for most people, sexual activity occurs in relationships.

Furthermore, studies have shown that attractive women retain value and are consistently approached romantically, regardless of age. This has been replicated by women who have successfully followed this blueprint to snatch "the bag", i.e. a desirable and financially stable partner—well into their 30's, 40's, 50's and beyond.

Clearly, men have an emotional investment in the "Red Pill" philosophy, regardless of data that debunks its tenets. The fact that these beliefs have stubbornly taken root to varying degrees in men's circles warrants examination rather than dismissal.

CHAPTER EIGHT

THE BACKGROUND

At one time, women in the Western world depended on men for their survival. They were consigned to working in the home, as wives and mothers to multiple children conceived before the advent of birth control (assuming she didn't die in childbirth). If they worked outside the home, they would earn a fraction of a man's salary for the same job. Women lucky enough to obtain an education were limited to certain professions, such as governesses or secretaries.

They were at the mercy of their husbands, fathers, or brothers, as they could not access credit, own property, or move freely without their consent.

Women were essentially trapped first by their kinfolk, and then by their husbands, due to financial necessity. This created a codependent dynamic between the sexes. Despite men resisting the "tender trap," they secretly yearned for the presence of a woman. Their needs extended beyond companionship and physical intimacy to include the emotional support and household management that women provided.

Their chauvinistic jokes about the "old ball and chain" concealed the significant truth: having a wife ENHANCED a man's emotional and physical well-being, extended his life expectancy, boosted his net worth, and elevated his overall happiness.

On the other hand, the data consistently showed that the happiest women are those who are single and childless, not married. What is behind this discrepancy? Firstly, women do not rely solely on their husbands as their emotional support. Regardless of a husband's presence in their lives, women are encouraged to openly express their emotions. They have a support system in place consisting of their mothers, sisters, and friends with whom they can discuss their situations. Furthermore, women are more inclined to seek professional assistance for mental health concerns.

Men, on the contrary, often keep their emotions bottled up. They typically only express comfort with expressing anger, which they may convey through aggression. Sharing their feelings is something they seldom do, even with their friends, with whom they tend to discuss more superficial topics.

For men, their life's pressure valve is loosened only in the presence of their wives, and not always in a positive way. Moreover, men place the burden on women for their emotional labor. His wife is the only person to whom he reveals his struggles. After they leave their mother's home, their wives' touch is often the only source of physical affection they receive. Unlike women's friendships, physical contact as innocuous as a hug between male friends is frowned upon.

Another unfortunate consequence of the stoic "lone wolf" facade is the tendency to eschew professional help when men are feeling sad, frustrated, or lonely.

When faced with negative emotions, some men seek solace in destructive behaviors like addictions to gambling, alcohol/drugs, and pornography. Instead of processing their feelings constructively, they may vent their frustrations by self-medicating or lashing out at their wives and children, both physically and emotionally.

In the most severe cases of mental instability, men may resort to committing suicide. Males die by suicide 3-4 times more so than females, underscoring the tragic consequences of isolation and loneliness that the emotionally weaker male sex is prone to.

CHAPTER NINE

THE OLD BALL AND CHAIN

Despite the obvious advantages that marriage yielded (longer life span, higher wages, better mental/physical health), wives were maligned as the "old ball and chain" - a tongue and cheek insult underscoring men's "loss" of freedom as they mourned the transition from bachelorhood to the commitments of married life.

Women's financial reliance on their husbands' wages emphasized the necessity of marriage as a survival mechanism, making it the primary purpose of such unions. This required women to stoke and maintain a man's affections to secure her well-being, using all the weapons in her arsenal (her beauty, sex appeal, and charm).

This dynamic reinforced the notion that women "captured" a partner in matrimony, becoming a prevailing cultural trope of the time.

No longer would a man enjoy the unrestricted freedom to travel the world, explore, date as many women as he liked, or spend his money solely at his discretion. From the instant the rings were swapped, and they crossed the threshold, a man's life ceased to be solely his own. He was now bound by the responsibilities as head of the household to his wife and future children--A heavy burden.

CHAPTER TEN
CHANGE IS INEVITABLE

The ideas of the enlightenment were a cornerstone of the American revolution and the political upheavals that spread throughout Europe. Liberty was a natural human right. Science and reason were promoted as the pathway to maximizing human potential. The infallibility of the church was questioned as the source of truth. Ancient views about the order of the world and the inequality of the class system were challenged.

However, it was not lost that these lofty ideals were not bestowed onto women or people of color. In the US, the "peculiar institution" remained intact throughout and after the war for Independence.

Despite the attempts of those in power to overlook these injustices, the gross inequities could not be ignored. The stark contrast between the equality advocated by founding fathers and the harsh realities faced by people of color and women reached a tipping point. Over time, persistent activism bore fruit, and equal rights became the birthright of every citizen.

Women secured the right to vote in 1919, but it took another 70 years for them to achieve superficial parity with men. Over this period, they gained access to bank accounts, credit and could purchase vehicles without the need for a husband or father as a co-signer. The introduction of birth control granted women control over their reproductive choices, empowering them to postpone or prevent motherhood according to their preferences. This newfound autonomy enabled them to make decisions about how to direct their energies, whether toward starting a family or pursuing a career.

CHAPTER ELEVEN
WOMEN'S LIB

Once Western women gained the ability to shape their own futures, how did they choose to exercise this newfound freedom?

Freed from reliance on a man's income, numerous women opted to forgo or postpone marriage in favor of building careers. They sought advanced education, traveled and explored different parts of the globe, purchased homes independently, ventured into entrepreneurship, engaged in investments, and fully embraced their capacity for self-expression.

At long last, women were free to choose; they could love men without any compulsion to marry, date multiple men simultaneously, and end relationships as they saw fit.

For those already in marriages, this newfound freedom had far-reaching implications. Husbands' less-than-chivalrous conduct was no longer tolerated merely out of economic necessity, leading to a corresponding increase in divorce rates.

Contrary to what the contemporary "Trads" may convey to their social media followers, life for women prior to the 1960s did not mimic a Norman Rockwell painting. These narratives might suggest that women spent their days leisurely lounging on couches and indulging in bonbons while their husbands toiled away, earning their coins with the sweat from backbreaking physical labor. In fact, the modern technology that reduced the workload in the home only became widespread after World War II, and even then, their access was restricted to the upper middle classes who could afford it.

Furthermore, these advances benefited husbands as much it benefitted wives, as machinery replaced much of the tedious, labor intensive, and dangerous tasks at work.

Furthermore, traditional life wasn't as perfect as the manosphere nostalgically depicts it. The same vices that persist today have always existed, but back then, wives often had no choice but to endure them or risk losing their financial support.

The misconduct hasn't changed. In the not-so-distant past, a "traditional" husband could indulge in adultery, solicit the services of prostitutes, squander his paycheck on gambling, backhand his children, and succumb to substance abuse—without pushback from his wife who was expected to "stand by her man".

Law enforcement often refrained from intervening in domestic disputes, considering them to be "family matters." Consequently, abuse often went unaddressed. Regrettably, this contributed to a legacy of dysfunctional family dynamics concealed beneath the facade of the ideal "Trad" family.

As women achieved financial independence, they were no longer compelled to compromise. They didn't have to turn a blind eye to their husband's infidelity, rightfully rejecting partners that put them at the risk of contracting STDs. They no longer had to track down their husbands in taverns, where family savings were frittered away on drinking and gambling. The need to hide knives, belts, or baseball bats before their husbands returned home to vent their work frustrations on the family (that they were charged to serve and protect) became a thing of the past.

It is no wonder that during this period, divorce rates soared. With their newly minted financial independence, women became unstoppable: able to provide for their families while protecting them from dysfunctional environments, creating the blueprint for limitless possibilities.

CHAPTER TWELVE

THE FALLOUT

This societal transformation had profound implications for dating. Women were no longer pressured to marry their high school sweethearts. They could pursue their education and establish careers before choosing a life partner. Women had the freedom to explore various relationships and engage in sexual experiences without the obligation of marriage. As reliable birth control became commonplace, sex was no longer restricted to marital unions.

Initially, it could be argued that men were the primary beneficiaries of this cultural shift. They no longer had to fear the anger of their girlfriend's father or face community disapproval as they sowed their oats. Pregnancy could now be effectively prevented, making sex a recreational activity with minimal consequences.

Dating evolved into a standalone pursuit, detached from the outcome of leading to marriage. The practice of dating to evaluate potential spouses became outdated. Couples engaged in dating for *fun* —entering into short-term and long-term relationships, ushering in an era of serial monogamy that supplanted the conventional courtship-to-marriage path.

Men were no longer compelled to marry to achieve sexual access. Instead, it sufficed to take a woman on a few dates, with the implicit understanding that physical intimacy was anticipated shortly after the third date.

Initially, this played to men's advantage, as they were no longer obligated to assume the roles of protector, provider, and steward to secure a consistent source of companionship and intimacy. However, after years of engaging in serial dating, a substantial number of men grew weary of moving from one relationship to another and desired to establish more stable, long-term connections.

Which woman should they select to become their bride and be worthy of them relinquishing their bachelor lifestyle?

These men held cherished memories of their high school and college sweethearts. It was a pure and innocent first love that left indelible marks on their hearts, even though they lacked the maturity and foresight to fully appreciate it at the time. They thought they would find many ladies to whom they could forge a deep connection, only to discover, years later, that authentic love was a rare jewel, and if not cherished, lost forever.

Some of these men yearned to rekindle that sense of first love with someone from their past. However, looking up their old flames on social media proved disheartening, as many of their former girlfriends had moved on and started families. To make matters worse, the ladies who were single didn't look exactly as they did in high school when they first caught their teenage eye crush's attention in study hall many years ago (lacking the self-awareness that they, too, no longer looked as they did in their youth!), which snuffed out the attraction.

Men were gripped by an existential panic. For millennia, it was customary for young couples to marry in their early to late twenties. Unfortunately, the extended adolescence subsidized by helicopter parents, birth control and red pill propaganda, kept men in denial to the harsh truth that women would not wait forever for them to be "ready". As they woke up in their 30's from their video game, processed food, doom scrolling slumber they were shocked to discover that the women in "peak fertility" who they were assured would be competing for their commitment, were running in the opposite direction.

In reality, when post wall men (a post-wall man is defined by those who are unable to effortlessly attract their desires as looks and status decline) attempted to pursue younger women, they were met with laughter and outright rejection. Women who were over 5 years younger than them typically displayed little interest in older men, leading to frustration and anger. Contrary to what the manosphere propagates, women consistently tend to favor men within their own age bracket, even as they age themselves.

Thus, younger American women were not considered viable options for marriage. Their lack of interest in older men romantically, coupled with their unpreparedness for marriage, made them unsuitable matches.

The logical choice (much to their horror) is to select partners from their immediate surroundings—those who share similar age/weight/ looks as well as similar academic and career circles. However, the typical Western male often holds an inflated opinion of himself. He fails to recognize that his options ARE within his league. Instead, he constantly aims above his league, operating in the delusion that they are on equal footing.

This delusion zone is the sweet spot for the third world girl. Your carefully curated responses to his courtship will not only inflate his ego like a hot air balloon but also secure you the bag like a Porsche Mom on a Black Friday spree. It's a bit like playing a game of "Let's Pretend" where he gets to be the hero in his own movie, and you're the Oscar-winning actress who knows just the right lines to say to keep the emotions running high and the cash flowing.

CHAPTER THIRTEEN

THE NUMBERS DON'T LIE

Demographic shifts are in line with these societal trends. The average age at first marriage has steadily risen, now standing at 30.5 for men and 28.6 for women.

Furthermore, as the age at first marriage has climbed, the overall marriage rate has DECLINED significantly. In fact, it has decreased by a staggering 60%! Back in 1970, the marriage rate stood at 76.5%, but by 2023, it had dropped dramatically to 31.1%.

Could the divorce rate of 40-50% for first marriages be part of the reason why people are gun shy about walking down the aisle?

Before the sexual revolution, it was often men who needed convincing to commit to marriage. However, in more recent times, American women have been the ones opting out altogether or delaying marriage until their late twenties.

Confronted with these conditions, men who were experiencing their first or second stint of singlehood began to explore alternative options in the dating scene.

Why should these self proclaimed high value men lower themselves to be with "roasties"? "Roasties" is their pejorative term for women over 30 whom they assume spent their twenties bouncing from the mattress of one attractive but unreliable "Chad" to another, neglecting the nice guys who treated them well in favor of handsome troublemakers.

(Ignoring the fact that these "roasties" didn't want them anyway

—if they played their cards right, the women they disparaged were already married.)

Rather than settling for "roasties," American men began to explore their options and seek potential partners from abroad. In the exotic and distant regions of Asia, Eastern Europe, or South America, they envisioned discovering a treasure trove: women who were fit, feminine, and submissive, eager to be captivated by an American knight in shining armor.

As smart women, why should we challenge their fantasies? No, our role is to capitalize on their misconceptions and GET THE BAG.

CHAPTER FOURTEEN

BODY COUNT

Western males, particularly incels, are obsessed with "body count." Their limited real-life experience with women, coupled with the prevalence of porn and OnlyFans, has led them to mistakenly believe that all Western women are promiscuous and "ran through".

They hold onto this belief even though an unprecedented number of people are experiencing a sexual drought.

The trend of decreased sexual activity, known as the "sexlessness epidemic," persists despite greater access to birth control, permissive attitudes about alternative lifestyles, and normalization of cohabitation without marriage.

Theoretically, meeting a potential mate should be easier than ever. Dating apps and social media give users an endless array of options to choose from. Interacting with filtered profiles via messenger or text rather than face to face minimizes the sting of rejection. Yet men report being lonelier than ever.

The ease of connection has ironically caused the average romance seeker to be lazy. It seems unfair that a life partner should not be deposited on one's doorstep like a food app delivery. More than ever, both men and women are dropping out of the dating scene altogether, frustrated by the shiny new thing syndrome.

The bros who are are "swiped left" upon by women who are out of their league bitterly gripe about the unsightly fatties they match with. Surely, all of the hot women of Tinder must be pooling together their sexual energy and taking numbers to have unbridled monkey sex with Chad!

However, the data shows a different picture. In fact, women are *less likely* to engage in casual sexual encounters compared to sex within committed relationships. This contradicts the Red Pill principle, which suggests that women, as the gatekeepers of sex, would engage in more unrestricted sexual activity if societal stigma were removed. Despite this, there is a misconception among some sexually frustrated men that women are engaging in such behavior. After all, if they could, they would!

The Red Pillers refer to this phase of female promiscuity as the "cock carousel". They posit that beautiful Staceys spend their teens and twenties jumping from one sexual encounter to another with "Chads", the attractive men who have unrestricted access to the booty call buffet.

It is only when women get close to their expiration date and are ready to retire from the cock carousel, that they settle down with beta cucks, push out a few children as a vehicle for 18 years of child support, and wait to divorce their husbands who have morphed into human ATM machines for their frivolous spending habits.

Women wait at the finish line and bang the winners. But not all women can get the winners.

Guess what category the "Passport Bros" and "Alphas" consider themselves?

CHAPTER FIFTEEN

THE PRIZE

The Manosphere has drummed it into their gullible audience's mind that they are the prize. A prize whose value increases as they grow older--whereas a woman's value decreases once she reaches "the wall".

"Men age like wine, women age like milk," the manosphere trumpets with homoerotic overtones, as they scour the internet for photos of handsome middle aged celebrities to gush over.

The gurus have bamboozled young men with the pipe dream that their prime doesn't arrive until midlife. They claim middle aged men retain their sex appeal AND have more to offer (namely, money) to the babes they desire compared to men within her age cohort. Hollywood has contributed to this lopsided social programming by casting films with out of shape old geezers with young and gorgeous starlets, conditioning men into believing that age gaps and looks gaps are the norm.

The manosphere advises young men to go into "monk mode" and wait their turn. At their sexual peak, young lads are redirected to focus on skill-building and financial portfolios instead of cold approaching—a convenient strategy to reduce competition!

It is scandalous that young men have, in their sexual prime, been brainwashed by their elders into avoiding women when they are at their horniest and hottest. The youth of today will never again possess the naturally robust muscle mass, thick and lustrous hair, or smooth and supple complexion that they do in their late teens and 20s. Yet the rhetoric has been so effective that the youth voluntarily castrate their desires for the promise of a harem in their dotage.

It's a testament to the potency of simpdom. Remember, it is in a man's DNA to simp. If he is not simping for a woman, that sexual napalm will be detonated elsewhere. Save divine intervention, the men who have been hypnotized by the RP's spell will become genetic dead-enders.

Regrettably, these young men's natural inclination to pursue their romantic interests has been co-opted by embittered old cynics. These so-called "mentors" resentfully acknowledge that they may never experience the joys of young love again (assuming they ever did). Consequently, they steer impressionable young men away from relationships precisely when young women their age are most likely to find them attractive. By removing the competition posed by these youthful contenders, they believe they can step in and pursue their own romantic interests with these same young women!

As a validation of their beliefs, they gleefully present charts showing that men tend to find women in their 20's most attractive, regardless of the men's age. Strangely, they overlook data indicating that women generally find men closer to their own age most attractive as *they* age.

Unsurprisingly, a 20-year-old woman finds men aged 20 to 23 most appealing. This preference for a narrow age gap of 1 to 3 years persists throughout a woman's life, as evidenced by marriage census data.

Nonetheless, the manosphere proliferates with revenge fantasies of the once beautiful and now remorseful Stacey decaying into the withered old crone contrasted with the bumper crop of barely legal teens vying for a chance to join middle aged Chad's harems.

These Penthouse Letter-esque delusions are echoed across social media, where RPers delight in sharing Reddit threads of "empty egg cartons" lamenting their fading looks and promiscuous pasts, which has relegated them to a state of loneliness accompanied by "wine and cats." These narratives seem tailored to fit the doomsday scenario predicted for attractive women who rejected the advances of "nice guys," leaving little doubt that the authors are frustrated men.

One of the accounts, "Women Posting Their L's," regularly features content that receives thousands of likes, often revolving around women's misfortunes. The comments section is filled with keyboard warriors proudly holding women accountable for their actions and even equating a woman's rejection of their advances to "violence." Ironically, these men seem to believe that they are exempt from their own karma.

In their worldview, they firmly believe that it is solely women who face scrutiny, while men escape unscathed despite squandering their youth on casual affairs, endless video games, and indulging in pornography.

CHAPTER SIXTEEN

IN LOVE AND GENDER WARS

A quick glance onto social media platforms will show you how cemented these concepts are in the manosphere. This is the misguided mindset of a man that goes overseas to find the love.

Because, despite the bravado, name-calling, and posturing about being an alpha man who is sick of American women's shit-- what they really desire, MORE than anything-- is a woman's love. If not her love, then they'll settle for her hate; for if they can make her feel SOMETHING, they have won.

Once a man has a woman's love, or her hate, the game is not over. It is up to her to choreograph the dance that will keep him addicted to her validation.

In many cases, Western women seem to have overlooked the fact that the brain is the body's largest sex organ. Instead of teasing, they jump straight into pleasing. Consequently, even after indulging in a full buffet at happy hour prices, men may find themselves pushing away from the table, still craving something beyond the menu, though unsure of what exactly that might be.

Despite their pride on being the logical sex, men are anything but. They can meet and sleep with women that meet all their criteria, but if she does not provide what he needs—the mystery, the chase, the tease—he will eventually tire of her, even if she is perfect on paper. The woman to whom he becomes hopelessly devoted is often not the hottest, tightest, or most submissive, but rather the one who inspires simpery.

This is why even beautiful and sweet women get dumped. She has failed to understand the male NEED to be manipulated, to serve, and submit. To be successful, she must "top" from the "bottom". In this dynamic, the male is a figurehead who is animated by her puppet strings. The neck controls the head. His actions are motivated by a desire to please and fulfill his wife.

Simping behavior is frequently ridiculed by other men because it strikes a chord with them. However, as we've explored, if a woman fails to channel this desire effectively, it will be redirected – to the manosphere, sports, or politics, for example. A woman who is not the object of her partner's simping is in for a life of poverty, misery and loneliness.

It is best for women to test early on to gauge a man's willingness to simp for them; if they are hopelessly married to the manosphere, religion, or politics, RUN!

CHAPTER SEVENTEEN
DON'T ARGUE WITH MEN

As you scroll through your social media feed, you'll come across women passionately debating against men who advocate for the repeal of the 19th Amendment. The RP Bros assert that feminism has caused the decline of Western civilization and predict dire outcomes from their liberation. Women who have bought into the boss babe narrative and postponed creating families for their careers will become empty, undesirable "egg cartons", nursing their sorrows with wine and antidepressants, they smugly claim. Women angrily reply and provide statistical data that shows that men "rope" (commit suicide) at a higher rate when they reach their midlife crisis.

Arguing with men is not only unproductive, but it is also unfeminine.

You will notice that not one man online has ever changed his mind about "the state of women today" as a result of online debates with women. If anything, they will dig their heels in deeper, despite any evidence you present that contradicts their beliefs.

Men will congregate, forming a hivemind with their friends, relishing the opportunity to bestow an "L" upon women. Unleashing harsh language that would surely make their mothers wince, they unload the vitriol the moment an online woman contradicts them. In that instant, she becomes the embodiment of all the women who ever rejected him, finally allowing him to settle the score.

From now on, adopt this rule: Only engage with men who can benefit you in some way; by fixing your tires, paying your phone bill, or covering your rent.

Everything else is a waste of time. The time you spend arguing with him energizes him. Any attention, even negative attention, galvanizes him!

Extract value or walk away.

Look at them as commodities. Engage only if you can get a return on your time investment.

CHAPTER EIGHTEEN
AGREE AND AMPLIFY

You may have observed that one of the most popular genres of twitter accounts with huge male followings is that of "Trad" e-girls. These are women that espouse a "traditional" lifestyle, that for the most part, is purely aesthetic.

Posting photos of themselves in modest (but body hugging or low cleavage) dresses and standing in fields of sunflowers, they humblebrag about the 5 course meals made from their organic farm harvest, pontificate about creating stable nuclear families with at least 5 children, and the importance of eschewing corporate indenture for life in domestic servitude to her family.

Meanwhile, many of these influencers are unmarried, divorced, childless, or single mothers—everything that their male audience claims to despise.

What these women have skillfully done is monetize male rage bait. These accounts capitalize on men's frustration at their inability to find girlfriends/wives by agreeing and amplifying red pill talking points.

The most popular twitter account at the moment is hosted by a post wall (age 26!), 6-foot tall non-chaste white woman. Pearl has carved out a niche for herself telling men what they want to hear, while not practicing what she preaches. She is educated, travels internationally, a career woman and has dated African American men (a common phobia that American white men have is that they will be cheated on inter-racially).

Pearl parrots the RP community bullet points, blaming feminism for the decline of morality, plummeting marriage rates, and the difficulty in supporting a family on one income. Women's freedom to choose their partners, access higher education, and exercise voting rights has pushed men to opt out of marriage.

These sentiments are liked and retweeted by her rapt audience of incels, who applaud like trained seals at a woman who "gets it" and rabidly defend her against anyone who dares question their queen.

What the redpillers conveniently overlook is that individuals like Pearl and those who share her views also benefit from and actively engage in the very privileges they argue should be revoked from women in a return to patriarchy.

Acting as a megaphone for the manosphere gives these women carte blanche to do as they please in private, while they trash modern women in public! Pearl votes, Pearl has had multiple sex partners, Pearl has a career—and the menfolk simp for her anyway!

This is the secret sauce to getting what you want from men. Weaving a fantasy that confirms their biases gives them cover to overlook everything you do that contradicts it. They will not care that you are divorced, a single mother, or an exotic dancer—as long as they find you somewhat attractive and tell them what they want to hear! You will be the arm candy that they can triumphantly parade around their ex-wives or co-workers.

You cannot argue a man out of his misogyny, but you can monetize it!

When you do meet your target, be it online or in person, you will apply this practice to your interactions. You will listen, act shocked and nod in sympathy as he tells you that "American women are trash" and complains about the lack of femininity, submissiveness, and chastity.

You will commiserate with his uphill battle in finding a good woman who hasn't been ruined by feminism. He bitterly recounts how entitled his ex-wife was, rewarding his hard work by refusing to put out, maxxing out credit cards and getting fat.

"It's a good thing that women from my country aren't that way," you chirp. "We like to treat our men like kings!"

This will melt him like butter on steamed corn. This is what he has been waiting for his whole life. Finally, a woman who gets it! A slim, trim, submissive low body count babe who worships the ground he walks on!

A woman's mission (if she accepts it) is to corral his contradictory opinions and to mold them to her (and her children's) benefit. Nodding her head yes as her husband waves philosophic about repealing the 19th while she gets her way and does whatever the hell she wants. Love her or hate her--that is exactly what Pearl and her ilk have mastered AND she gets paid.

CHAPTER NINETEEN

THE UNICORN

He has never felt this way about any girl before. Despite knowing you only briefly, he can already feel himself falling in love with you. You hang on to his every word as he spins tall tales while treating you to a gourmet dinner (thanks to the generous currency exchange rate); he even buys you roses from a street vendor on a romantic impulse. When you mention needing to end the date early due to a pending phone service cutoff, he quickly wires the funds to ensure your connection continues uninterrupted.

He can hardly believe his luck that this attractive young lady is paying attention to him. It is the exact opposite of the way college girls reacted to him in the States – calling him a gross and dirty old man – not even giving him a chance to prove how cool and hip he is! If he's on the younger side, he'll be amazed at how nonjudgmental you are about his fashion choices and awkward mannerisms—qualities that his female classmates frequently ridiculed him for.

In truth, you may not even be more than a "5" on the looks scale —but your exotic flair, slender physique, and baby voice instantly elevates you in his eyes and tents his pants.

Like the online female RP allies, you may have had children, "hit the wall" (over 35), or have a menial or sex work related job. On the surface, you bring nothing to the table-- however, you are given a special status by virtue of your serendipitous alignment to his red pill ideology. You become a unique find in his eyes, a rare breed that "understands it all" — a unicorn, if you will, a rare treasure in a distant land.

Make him feel loved and understood, while stoking but never satisfying his horniness.

Slowly reveal your troubled circumstances, without venturing into the complaint zone. Breathlessly tell him about the high price of rent; the rising cost of utilities; the long commute that takes two buses and a train ride to get to your low paying job; your sick mother that you care for without the help of your siblings.

Sigh and use your baby voice to describe how you do your best to care for those you love. At this point he will volunteer to ease your burden. You deserve it! You are not entitled like American girls who sit at cushy desk jobs taking orders from their corporate boss instead of a husband at home.

Voila! You have successfully established the precedent for a financial relationship with your admirer. He is deeply captivated by you, considering you a woman entirely distinct from those he encountered back in his home country. A woman who wants him for him!

What he doesn't realize, however, is that you are not fundamentally dissimilar from the American women he despises. Just like all women, you have essentially adhered to the traditional norm of seeking financial stability: The Gold Standard.

CHAPTER TWENTY

ALL RELATIONSHIPS ARE TRANSACTIONAL

In an effort to combat the hookup culture than has poisoned American society, dating coaches have unveiled the "90 Day Rule" to weed out incompatible partners.

As we have previously discussed, jumping into intimacy within the first month of dating has proven to be disastrous for women. Oxytocin, the cuddling hormone, hijacks her decision-making skills. Thanks to a taste of skin to skin contact, she feels bonded to a man with whom she shares no values, morals or common goals.

Enter the 90 day rule, a strategy for women to vet prospects with a modicum of detachment. During the probationary period, lasting for the first 90 days of dating, potential couples are advised to steer clear of kissing, sexual activity, or exclusivity. This gives them ample time to analyze red and green flags, while debating the yellow flags.

While we feel this is an improvement over the situationships and friends with benefits arrangements that have dominion over the contemporary dating landscape, it doesn't go far enough.

Pumping the breaks on nookie is a good start. To truly gauge her suitor's sincerity, she should set up a series of financial benchmarks that he must meet. Forget the 90 day rule; women should implement a $10,000 dollar rule. Her romantic prospects do not have to drop the benjamins all at once, but over the course of the courtship, he should be steadily depositing money into her coffers. The investment can take the form of cash, gifts, or jewelry.

What about whisking you away for vacations, you may wonder? While treating you to a holiday getaway demonstrates some measure of generosity, it is a gesture that benefits him immensely. Therefore, the dollar amount he spends on travel does not factor into the $10,000 dollar threshold. Particularly since he can use credit card points for flights and hotels at little or no cost to himself!

Vacationing together allows him to enjoy the perks of traveling to resorts, fine dining and excursions, all while having uninterrupted time with you without an easy escape route and cockblocking chaperones. On the surface, couples trips are a way for him to give the impression that he is spoiling you, when in fact he is rubbing his hands together in anticipation of sharing a room with you overnight.

CHAPTER TWENTY-ONE
FORGET THE 90 DAY RULE

In an effort to combat the hookup culture that has poisoned American society, dating coaches have unveiled the "90 Day Rule" to weed out incompatible partners.

As we have previously discussed, jumping into intimacy within the first month of dating has proven to be disastrous for women. Oxytocin, the cuddling hormone, hijacks her decision-making skills. Skin to skin contact creates bonds to men with whom she shares no values, morals or common goals.

Enter the 90 day rule, a strategy for women to vet prospects with a modicum of detachment. During the probationary period, lasting for the first 90 days of dating, potential couples are advised to steer clear of kissing, sexual activity, or exclusivity. This gives them ample time to analyze red and green flags, while debating the yellow flags.

While we feel this is an improvement over the situationships and friends with benefits arrangements that have dominion over the contemporary dating landscape, it doesn't go far enough.

Pumping the breaks on nookie is a good start. But to truly gauge her suitor's sincerity, she should set up a series of financial benchmarks that he must meet. Forget the 90 day rule; women should implement a $10,000 dollar rule. Her romantic prospects do not have to drop the benjamins all at once, but over the course of the courtship, he should be steadily depositing money into her coffers. The investment can take the form of cash, gifts, or jewelry.

(Our TWG are advised to implement this rule as well, in USD currency! It will be easy for him to pretend he is a Rockefeller on your home turf when the exchange rate allows him to buy you a gourmet meal for the price of a coffee and pastry in America. Exceptions may apply if you need to immigrate ASAP—but he needs to foot the legal bills for your visa and moving costs, at the minimum.)

What about whisking you away for vacations, you may wonder? While treating you to a holiday getaway demonstrates some measure of generosity, it is a gesture that benefits him immensely. Therefore, the dollar amount he spends on travel does not factor into the $10,000 dollar threshold. Particularly since he can use credit card points for flights and hotels at little or no cost to himself!

Vacationing together allows him to enjoy the perks of traveling to resorts, fine dining and excursions, all while having uninterrupted time with you without an easy escape route and cockblocking chaperones. On the surface, couples trips are a way for him to give the impression that he is spoiling you, when in fact he is rubbing his hands together in anticipation of sharing a room with you overnight.

A key aspect of this fiduciary hurdle is that he spends his money on you in ways that do not directly benefit him. This is crucial for you to snare him psychologically. By paying your bills, your tuition, your rent, and buying you jewelry, clothing, and property, he is investing in your well being in the hopes that it will hopefully pay off, some day. But it might not. It is a risky move for him. The more he spends, the less likely he is to walk away.

And even if he does walk away, so what? If he wakes up one day and decides you are not the one for him, you still come out ahead. The diamond earrings, designer purses and new iPhone he gifted while in the throes of passion will console you as you cross him off and add another candidate to your roster.

This is a practice that will benefit TWG and Western ladies alike . As we have mentioned previously, the feeling of being cheated, of wasting time, and needing closure is a direct result of over-investing. We guarantee that if you step back and allow the gentleman to trade *their* currency ($$$) for your beauty currency at an exchange rate that you have predetermined-- you won't need to chase him down to ask why the relationship ended. It's a win-win for you, whether he stays or he goes.

That said, we do believe that the 90 day has some value, but without the $10,000 dollar rule, it lacks teeth. Therefore, we advise that our clientele adopt both tactics. TWG should wait until marriage regardless, as your conservative upbringing gives perfect cover for abstinence until the ring exchange. We believe American girls should also abstain until marriage, but if you must insist on sampling before buying, satisfy the $10,000 rule first.

CHAPTER TWENTY-TWO

INSTATHOTS AND THE GOOD GIRLS

As your vet your suitors for a deeper relationship, you may observe that his social media stances do not reflect his offline behavior.

Look no further than his follow list for the most glaring examples of online hypocrisy. He may follow RP accounts that relish in mudslinging women while SIMULTANEOUSLY following the accounts of Instagram "thots": scantily clad women who seductively pose and demand tribute from their salivating fans. Though they claim to despise attention seeking "hoez", they cannot seem to drag their eyes (or their wallets) away from their gyrating physiques.

You may even discover he has an Only Fans subscription. Do not be surprised if he spends half the day on twitter insulting "INSTATHOTS" and the other half watching OF and sending them money for nudes.

What you should not do is call him out on this two-faced behavior during the courtship phase. YET. Once you have him firmly by the balls (and the wallet), you can start to impose restrictions on him. You may not even need to address this, as the more you monopolize his heart and mind, he will naturally gravitate away from this pixelated outlet for his loneliness.

That said, you can learn a lot from a man's hypocrisy. What a man says he wants versus what he pursues and falls in love with are two different things.

Men pontificate about wanting a good Christian girl with good values, yet, if they do not pass his attraction test, they are invisible to him.

You may have noticed this in your own house of worship. The pretty and extroverted girls are picked first while the mousy and plain girls are picked last, if at all. It doesn't matter how devout or moral they are on the inside if they are not bubbly and cute on the outside.

The same dynamic happens in the USA. Men filter women by what passes their attraction threshold, then select for values. However, many men are so desperate for companionship that they will overlook a woman's toxicity entirely if a halfway decent looking woman pays attention to them. This works in our favor, ladies!

A useful guideline is to cast a jaundiced eye to when men grandstand online or to their friends about their supposedly high standards. Many of the "red flags" they insist are grounds for "nexting" are often just virtue signaling meant to impress their peers. Privately, it's clear that those standards don't hold much weight.

You, on the other hand, will do the inverse. You will pretend that your standards are low, while actually setting the bar high. On your profile, you will say that you are looking for a "kind hearted gentleman with good values; age, height and weight unimportant". This will immediately set you apart from the "biotches" who, in their estimation, ignore the nice guys to date Chads: 6 feet tall, making 6 figures, with at least a 6 in the family jewels department.

It will feel like a breath of fresh air to speak to a woman to whom he doesn't have to lie about his age/height/hairline/age. Thanks to RP teachings, middle aged or dorky men are convinced they age like wine and look great for their age, despite their huge guts, ED, and receding hairlines. Therefore, they feel entitled to women who are younger and/or better looking than they are.

Deep down, he wants to be admired by the lady he lusts after. Your receptivity to older, chubby and/or nerdy men like him serves as a reassuring pacifier, affirming his worldview.

What he doesn't need to know is that you are discretly screening, but not strictly for "love". You are screening for a love that motivates a man to give you shekels *and* take the leap and marry you. He doesn't need to know that your love for him is contingent on the ring, but he will soon learn you mean business if he attempts to drag his feet.

Do not worry if his friends and family warn him about foreign women--once he is in love, their objections will fall on deaf ears.

As far as he is concerned, you love HIM for HIM, unlike all the shallow American girls who rejected him for being too old, too fat, not romantic enough, or too stingy.

At this juncture, your material needs must be a given, seamlessly integrated into the fabric of the relationship. As you provide a steady stream of admiration and validation to your emotionally and sexually starved partner, it will bring him joy and pride, making him believe that he's the sole source of your happiness.

His manhood is restored.

CHAPTER TWENTY-THREE

ALL MEN ARE SIMPS

Men will also spend a lot of time mocking other men who they label as simps.

They define a simp as a man who is so desperate for a woman's love that he will humiliate himself for a crumb of affection, even if he never gets the "cookie".

The term "simp" has been extrapolated from its original context. It is now hurled at a man who is nice to any woman, including his wife!

On social media, observe the comments when a man posts about helping his 8-month pregnant wife with chores, shares pictures of the engagement ring he purchased for his fiancée, or divulges a plan to arrange a dream vacation to Disneyworld for his girlfriend, who missed out on the experience as a child. You'll often find a barrage of insults in the replies, labeling him as a "simp."

The incel (involuntary celibates) will tag their favorite manosphere guru, hoping that he will notice his fanboying and give him validation. If the incel says something that inadvertently conflicts with his manosphere mentor, he will apologize obsequiously.

By calling men who respect and care for their partners "simps" the RP acolyte hopes to get a high five and pat on the back from his RP bros. Which is not abstaining from simping at all. In essence, he is actually simping for the RP community itself!

It is in a man's nature to "simp" for something; in absence of a woman to spoil, he will worship at the altar of another man that he idolizes.

There is an order of operations. If they aren't directly immersed in the manosphere, they idolize and simp for self-help coaches, fitness/ bodybuilding experts, sports teams, or political movements. They may even become radicalized by religion.

However, none of these substitutes can compare to the lost paradise, the garden of Eden he viscerally returns to when he simps for a woman. It is a return to the womb, to his most vulnerable state, where all of creation begins. With his head in a woman's lap, his emotional life in her delicate hands, he is home. It is the source of his bliss and his shame. And so, the weaker man will cosplay disdain for what he so desires the most.

Not so for the true Alpha men. Throughout history, the most powerful men have simped for their beloveds. In fact, the women they obsessed over were neither under 25, nor virginal, nor naive! Great men like Napoleon, who adored Josephine, a single mother who was 6 years his senior and had a mouthful of rotten teeth. Byzantine Emperor Justinian made an Empress out of Theodora, a former prostitute. These formidable women did not conform to the ideals of femininity yet their men unabashedly simped nonetheless.

We TWG are on a mission to transform the perception of simping from a pejorative to a positive. Simpdom should be celebrated, not condemned. We are promoting a broader conversation on the true definition of masculinity—one that empowers men to engage in healthy and supportive relationships for their beloved without ridicule or judgment.

How to distinguish between a simp and a waste of oxygen? As you vet for the appropriate mark, you will need to keep emotionally detached (this can be accomplished by talking to several men at the same time – more on building a roster, later) to see if your feminine presence will inspire him to shift away from his incel pursuits and begin simping for you.

Keep in mind, Truly Wonderful Girls (TWGs), don't resort to nagging to induce change in men; instead, we ignite transformation through our feminine presence. By presenting ourselves as damsels in distress with crises only they can resolve, and dispensing intermittent doses of our love, we tap into the inherent "simping" behavior encoded in a man's DNA.

The chances that he will begin simping for you, if you play to his emotions and biases, are high. If he does not, ruthlessly cut him loose. Do waste time trying to convince him.

Only choose the man that will simp for YOU.

CHAPTER TWENTY-FOUR
THE GIRLFRIEND LIMBO

American women see dating as a way find an eligible man with whom they feel a "spark" and thus fall in love. They slog through an assembly line of coffee dates to snare a boyfriend, a simulated husband who gets all of the benefits of marriage without having any legal responsibilities. It is a quasi-committed situationship which will keep her off the market while giving her male companion exclusive access to her body. These forever girlfriends want to eventually marry but have resigned themselves to months or years of serial dating that may or may not yield a walk down the aisle.

American women believe they must give up the "cookie" within a month(!) or risk losing their potential boyfriend. You read that right: they have not even broached the topic of exclusivity, and yet she is being pressured to be intimate with a virtual stranger. Consequently, it's not surprising that women often don't find much enjoyment in such rushed sexual encounters.

However, the first of many problems with this arrangement arises when she forms emotional attachments to a man who may not have been particularly special to begin with. Jumping into bed before taking the time to examine his values and core qualities obscures her better judgment. Sexual intimacy creates a fragile bond that can make it difficult to end a relationship with a man who clearly isn't right for her. This sudden neediness can often result in her losing her leverage in the relationship.

She finds herself in the dreaded "girlfriend limbo," a

perplexing state of relationship purgatory where she's neither fully free nor officially married. It's like being trapped in a pathetic rom-com sans the happily ever after-- nervously biting her fingernails and clinging to the hope that by avoiding any form of pressure, she might someday receive that elusive ring she's been yearning for.

CHAPTER TWENTY-FIVE
DATING IS A BUSINESS

While the Western woman's missteps may inadvertently make it easier for TWG's to stand out, I don't intend to be flippant. Despite the attention-grabbing title of my book, my genuine desire is for all women to thrive. To any American women reading this, I strongly urge you to reconsider your approach to selecting a life partner.

You must look at love in a different light.

"Falling" in love is the most foolish choice a woman can make. Falling in love is why it hurts so much when it fails. You did not look both ways before you crossed the street. You fell flat on your face and played yourself.

The time you invested making him dinners, cleaning his house and Netflix and chillin' should have been spent going on dates (on his dime), being courted and actively planning for a shared future rather than adopting a "let's see how it goes" approach.

You should have assembled a squad of eager suitors, each competing for your heart like contestants on a dating game show. Picture it: your very own "Love Olympics" with bachelors battling it out for your attention, complete with scorecards and dramatic eliminations, instead of putting all your romantic hopes into one fragile basket of love.

When it ends you are angry. Angry at him--and angry at yourself. You want to cuss him out for the time and money and emotional labor you wasted on this dude for months or years with nothing to show for it!

As the modern American girlfriend, you might have believed you were acting in a "fair" and "progressive" manner when you agreed to split bills evenly, allowed him personal freedom, refrained from pressuring him into marriage, and made physical intimacy readily available on demand.

Only to discover that the surplus he hoarded by going 50/50 with you was reallocated to the girls he met online and at the club! The benjamins he saved by going halfsies with you were tucked into the lace of another girl's g-string. A girl who is not as educated, pretty, cultured or accomplished as you are. Ironically, she is the type of girl he mocked as a "thot"!

You are outraged and you want closure. Why did he play you like this? When you treated him like a king and devoted the prime years of your life to him?

The reason you want closure is because you gave more to the relationship than he did. Your former flame easily washed his hands of your so-called relationship and walked away with a smile, because he scored you at a basement bargain price by being your "boyfriend"!

Don't fall for the okie-doke. The "girlfriend" title is nothing more than a convenient way to ensure your sexual loyalty while he explores his options, guilt-free. There are no guarantees that you will have anything to show for your years of non-legally binding exclusivity.

Do not date aimlessly. Be courted with intention.

What western women have forgotten is to view dating as a business. Would you keep showing up for work if you weren't being paid? Would you allow your boss to string you along with empty promises to compensate you as you bust your hump week after week?

Nah! Yet you, the modern American woman, have "submitted" to sexual communism. It's time to stop giving every comrade who stands at the bread line his ration of intimacy for the year!

CHAPTER TWENTY-SIX
LOVE YOURSELF FIRST

My American friends, you are inverting the natural order by "falling" in love with men at first blush. Love yourself first. Give yourself an abundance of love. A woman who loves herself is highly attractive, radiant and magnetic. When you prioritize yourself, it will act as a repellent to unworthy men!

A woman can only receive the amount of love that she has for herself. A woman who is the VIP of her life and loves herself unconditionally magnetizes men who cherish her the way she cherishes herself. On the other hand, self-hatred will be mirrored in the negligent, abusive, unfaithful men she chooses.

Do a post-mortem of your relationships. Is your love roster a mass produced assembly line of dusties, scrubs and ne'er do wells? Looking back, you likely felt a soulmate/twin flame connection with these subpar scrotes who did little or nothing for you. Yet you tolerated the bare minimum because of "chemistry" while ignoring men who were stable, consistent, and even tempered.

Or perhaps you never felt much chemistry with your dusty exes – but you were guilted into "building" up a man with potential, lest you be labeled a gold- digger. Only to find yourself ultimately empty-handed and exhausted as their potential failed to materialize, and their lack of advancement began to affect your credit score and create disparities in your social standing?

It does you a disservice to point the finger at bare minimum men who need fixing, mothering, and mentoring, when you chose to give your body and your heart where your efforts were not reciprocated.

Take ownership of your mistakes. Understand that it was your lack of self-love, perhaps born from a troubled childhood, that led you to accept neglect, mistreatment, and broken promises as ordinary! Society conditions women to be "nice" and accommodating of men's shortcomings, under the false notion that having any relationship, even a dysfunctional one, was better than being alone!

Be brutally honest with yourself. If the only men you allowed into your space are those who denied you the princess treatment, it is because deep down, you believed you were unworthy of anything better.

Ironically, bending your rules and compromising your values to "get the guy" made your boyfriend lose respect for you. The "why buy the cow when the milk is free" cliché is part of the national lexicon for a reason.

Let yourself cry. Grieve the dead flowers, but do not water them. When the mourning period is over, it's time for reinvention. Say goodbye to the woman who was drawn to and/or accepted lackluster treatment.

Though you may not be that woman yet, fake it until you make it! From this point forward, deprive the parasites of a host. Refuse to give your lifeblood to another bottom feeder.

Don't neglect the external aspect of self-improvement. Work on enhancing your physical well-being alongside your inner growth. Go to the gym and engage in regular exercise. Nourish yourself with nutritious foods. Elevate your appearance and style. Surround yourself with a circle of friends who uphold high standards and are actively advancing in their lives.

Love every cell in your body. Love the parts of your body you are ashamed of.

The parts you critique the most? Send love and approval to them: your stomach that didn't bounce back after pregnancy; the scars on your arms from when you self-harmed as a teen; the fingernails you have bitten down when you are anxious and afraid.

Love the experiences you disown: the child you had out of wedlock; the lack of college degree; the divorce from a dusty whose red flags you ignored.

When you ruminate over your perceived mistakes and flaws, you are your own bully. Stop beating yourself up. Practice forgiveness—when you know better, you do better. Giving in to guilt and shame subconsciously keeps your blessings away!

Letting go of self-loathing and sending love and approval to everything in your personal world (the "good" and the "bad") will remove resistance to the stuff you really want out of life.

Try it. Every morning, look at yourself in the mirror and say, "I love and approve of you, (name).

As you grow to love yourself from the inside out, the 3D outer world will reflect your new inner reality. Your depth of self-love will determine the love you receive from others.

It is beyond the scope of this brief guide, but I will expand upon how to truly cultivate self-love in a subsequent book in this series. We will also go in depth about the power of forgiveness. Forgiving ourselves, and the people and events that wronged us, is a powerful practice that clears out negative energy and creates a path for abundance and peace.

For now, let us examine how love is demonstrated by the givers, the masculine, and how it is received, by us, the feminine.

CHAPTER TWENTY-SEVEN
LOVE IS ACTION

Ladies, take heed: true love is not a feeling. It is a DOING. It is not butterflies in your stomach (which is often your nervous system's way of warning you that someone is toxic), nor the way he kisses you (transitory lust) or his swagger (inversely proportional to his crippling insecurities).

True love is manifested through tangible actions such as covering your expenses, purchasing a car for you, adding your name to property deeds, and appointing you as a beneficiary of his life insurance policy. When a man loves, he provides. No exceptions.

You will see how you are measured in a man's eyes by the way he treats you from the very first date.

Do you think he would ask his dream girl for a walk in the park, a cup of coffee, or an ice cream cone? Would he ask a Margot Robbie, Ashley Graham or Zendaya (whomever his ideal is) lookalike out for a happy meal?

Absolutely not! He would be working tirelessly to woo her.

You may think you are vetting him on the first date to see if he is boyfriend material. What you fail to realize is that he is also vetting YOU!

The lukewarm suitor is not trying to impress you. It's a number game. He is testing to see if you will settle for the bare minimum from him. All the while you invest the money and effort to look good – wearing makeup, heels, perfume and a cute dress!

Do not allow yourself to be guilted by equal rights propaganda into splitting the check. You are doing HIM a disservice by emasculating him, even if he is the one that suggested going Dutch.

Men don't know what they want. He will say he likes a woman that brings something to the table and splits expenses. He will push to cohabit before marriage to "test drive" the relationship.

Yet, despite women complying with his demands for a 50/50 split in responsibilities, his history is littered with a graveyard of defunct relationships. He overlooks the possibility that his refusal to simp contributes to the recurring pattern of failure.

Years pass and Ms. Mommy bang-maid has graduated and earned her wifey diploma after years of playing house. Naturally, her priorities shift from self-care to child-care once she births his children. Her body has gone through a dramatic change. At this point her husband starts to express dissatisfaction with the reduced effort she puts into her appearance, seeing it as a personal affront. He doesn't see his reluctance to pitch in as a factor in her exhaustion and decreased libido. Nevertheless, he expects wifey to shoulder the entirety of household chores, tend to the needs of the children, and maintain a full-time job.

Regrettably, splitting responsibilities equally can disrupt the balance of masculine and feminine polarity in a relationship. When a woman is compelled to juggle her career, household management, and childcare simultaneously, she often leans into her masculine energy. The mental and emotional labor required in this situation can prevent her from fully embracing her feminine energy and finding moments of rest within it.

This upheaval of the natural order has serious repercussions. The pressure to perform across mental, emotional, and physical domains can take a toll on you, the modern American woman. It might manifest in weight gain and reduced attention to personal grooming. The toll of sleepless nights can become evident in the lines etched onto your forehead and bags under your eyes.

When a man is unable or unwilling to fulfill the fundamental roles of being a provider and protector, it can give rise to feelings of resentment. Instead of introspection, he might find it easier to place the blame on his woman.

Once the bubbly, carefree girl he fell in love with is too stressed with working to pay bills and soothing crying children to baby his needs, he may see it as a permission slip to seek gratification elsewhere. It won't occur to him to ease her burden, as he is now reliant on her unpaid labor to make his hours of gaming, napping on the couch and hanging out with his beer buddies possible. Watching porn/OnlyFans when exhaustion kills her libido makes perfect sense to him. Chatting with women online and embarking on an emotional affair with a stranger is easier than addressing the uneven dynamic at home. He may rationalize crossing the line into infidelity, believing it's a just response to her neglect of his needs.

Once the infidelity is revealed and the wife, depleted from bearing the sole burden of home responsibilities and chores, reaches her breaking point, the betrayal of her husband's infidelity cuts even deeper. The couple then parts ways, leaving a fractured family in their wake.

As we have discussed previously, men often avoid taking responsibility for the breakdown of their marriages, instead blaming feminism and the entitled women it supposedly created. They forget that it was feminism that granted them access to no-strings-attached third-date sex and 50/50 dates in the first place!

Ironically, this is when the divorced man (or the bachelor who is ready to hang up his spurs) looks abroad for the perfect wife. The one who rests in her feminine and allows him to actualize his masculinity and provide 100%.

This scenario played on repeat should convince the American woman of the folly of modern dating. A woman who brings everything to the table will lose everything-- including the table.

American women mistakenly believe that because they can be coerced into falling in love with gifts, acts of service, and kindness with men they are not initially interested in dating, that men operate the same way.

News flash: Men do not fall in love the way women do! If he is not smitten with you from the start, no amount of effort will convince him that you are his dream girl. By cooking elaborate meals, using your connections to advance his career, and providing acrobatic sex on demand, you will only become a placeholder, nothing more. He might even marry you for your Herculean efforts, but make no mistake, you will stay in the masculine space and continue to provide for the duration of the relationship until it combusts.

Therefore, all women should make it a priority to stay in the feminine receptive role. Release the guilt you have been conditioned to feel when receiving gifts, money, and favors from men. It is your birthright as a woman.

If the men who swipe right on your profile balk at what they see as your lack of effort and standards, let them ghost. You are worth a Chanel, not a coffee. Continue screening until the prince appears who places the glass slipper on your foot and treats you like the princess that you are.

CHAPTER TWENTY-EIGHT

GROW IN LOVE

We will repeat this over and over again until your brain is reprogrammed.

Falling in love is masculine. A man's gender ideology gets tossed into the trash bin when he meets "the one." Blood flow to his brain is redirected south and his body becomes a life support system for his desire to possess her.

Conversely, when a woman makes the mistake of "falling" in love, she is knocked off her pedestal. She becomes mortal. A woman who immediately capitulates at the onset of lovebombing and future faking is demoted from the trophy bride to the booby prize as a result of her fall from grace.

As women, we GROW in love. We do not give our love until it is earned.

We caution our mentees that while we advocate detachment during the getting to know you phase, this does not meet you should act cold and bitchy. On the contrary! You should act sweet, laugh at his jokes, and be attentive as he spins his stories.

Smile as he outlines plans for a future for you and your future homestead but do not get sucked into the fantasy. You will not act cold, but your feelings will be "cold" until they are warmed up by his actions that demonstrate he will provide and protect.

CHAPTER TWENTY-NINE

WOMEN ARE THE GATEKEEPERS OF SEX...AND RELATIONSHIPS

In modern relationships, men have used reverse psychology to brainwash women into believing that while women control the frequency of sex, men are the gatekeepers of relationships.

This lopsided dynamic is imposed when the man assumes the role of the "prize" to be won over by stripper pole moves, home cooked meals, and willingness to "Netflix and Chill". In this scenario the lady goes overboard in pretending to be the laid back "cool girl" who is accepting of low-effort dates—while she secretly gnashes her teeth wondering if she has done enough to earn his commitment or if she's just another pump-n-dump!

This sad state of affairs creates anxiety in a woman as she tap-dances and smiles through the pain of her situationship's whims. She has bought into the narrative that as his future "ball and chain", she must convince him she is worth giving up his swinging bachelorhood, his nights out with his homies, and most of all, the other women who are chomping at the bit for a chance to be with him.

Sounds comical, doesn't it? Yet so many women have fallen for the gender bait and switch. They have given away their power. Their mad pursuit puts men in receptive mode, which keeps American women on their toes, instead of the other way around!

You cannot "out-nice" a poor self concept. If women believe that men are the gatekeepers of commitment, they will never stop auditioning. Viewing marriage as the ultimate achievement, they will sideline their wants and needs in pursuit of the ring.

A woman who constantly vies for men's affections will grow weary and irritable—unlike men who thrive in competitive situations. Over time, men too will grow weary and irritable, from being denied the opportunity to win over the woman of their dreams. Despite enjoying the flattery of women chasing them, they will never feel quite fulfilled by what is not earned.

A man who's been excessively pampered, instead of appreciating a woman's efforts, will push the envelope and misbehave. This behavior can manifest in many ways, such as ignoring her texts, showing disrespect in public and private, and declaring that he's "not being ready for a relationship". This is the reward a woman receives for serving herself up a platter for him to sample free or charge.

It's evident that disrupting the natural order leads to the chaos we witness today. Here's the stark reality: a woman's existence holds more value than a man's in terms of reproductive fitness. If 90% of men were to vanish, humanity would endure, aided by scientific advancements.

You wield the power to bring forth life, shaping the legacy of future generations. Your ability to create life is unmatched, making you a pure source of energy.

The importance of our presence is underscored when observing how a man's life can unravel when they have lost a wife or girlfriend. Without her guiding light their existence may feel hollow until they find a new partner to fill the void.

If women collectively decided to assert their boundaries, the landscape would shift dramatically. By closing the gates and reclaiming control over their bodies, wombs, and attention, women could catalyze profound change. This isn't just about individual actions; it's a call for a collective awakening to recognize the strength and value of women everywhere.

CHAPTER THIRTY

STOP THE INSANITY

To our American audience: it doesn't have to be this way. You have the power. There is a goldmine between your legs. It's time to guard your pumpum like Fort Knox. Don't give it away for free.

Born in America, you're the luckiest women in the world. You have the freedom to pursue education, chase your aspirations, cast your vote, and travel without hindrance. It's time to seize these opportunities fully.

Which way forward, Western woman?

Now, back to our regularly scheduled programming....

CHAPTER THIRTY-ONE
THE CANDIDATES

But first, we must separate the wheat from the chaff. Our American readers will recognize these profiles from their reject pile.

This pool of suitors are the men most likely to search for love overseas. These candidates may have overlapping characteristics, but generally speaking, they will fall into the following cohorts.

1. The Incel.
2. The Divorce'
3. The Aging Bachelor
4. The Hobosexual

CHAPTER THIRTY-TWO
THE INCEL

The incel is a different breed of male. "Incel" is short for involuntary celibate, an online subculture of men that feel entitled to but cheated out of sexual relationships with attractive women due to their insurmountable standards. Unlikely to seek professional help for their mental health, their feelings of hopelessness and despair have led to the formation of the incel as an identity rather than a temporary circumstance.

The incel movement is characterized by misogyny, with their members directing vitriol towards women whom they perceive as having an unfair advantage in the sexual marketplace. They often attribute their own romantic struggles to female hypergamy, the idea that women seek out mates of higher social status, and view this as a form of sexual injustice. Consequently, they regard the deprivation of sex and love from lower-status men as a form of oppression.

The typical incel is a man under 35, often with right-wing leanings, who may or may not be gainfully employed. They frequently spend their spare time online, engaging in activities such as gaming or expressing anger towards "Stacey" - a term used to describe fit, attractive women who hold the power to determine which men receive romantic attention. In the incel worldview, "Chad" represents tall, handsome, and successful men who are the winners in the sexual marketplace, leaving those at the bottom rung of the social hierarchy condemned to a life of celibacy.

One popular belief in the manosphere is that 80% of women

compete for the top 20% of men, with the top tier being defined by their wealth, looks, and social status. By this reasoning, the remaining 80% of men are left to vie for the attention of the bottom 20% of women. According to this perspective, many women would prefer to be "pumped and dumped" by highly desirable Chads than pursue more meaningful connections with men deemed less attractive ("sub 5s" on a scale of 1 to 10).

Incels bully women online for being shallow gold-diggers unwilling to humble themselves to date a "nice guy" like themselves. Ironically, incels steadfastly refuse to lower their own standards and date obese roasties.

Despite his online woman-hating persona, the incel, who in real life, is often anti-social and riddled with anxiety, harbors an intense yearning for connection. His community of romantic rejects functions as a substitute of sorts, validating their shared victimhood by reposting Reddit stories about "women taking the L" (women taking a loss) as they heap insults and slurs on the "thots".

Beyond their grievances against women who have the audacity to enforce boundaries and have prerequisites, these incels hunger to be loved unconditionally, as their mothers loved them.

Like the older divorced men, these incels are ripe for the picking. They have been fomenting a sense of anger at the unsuitability of the women in the dating marketplace. They are convinced no American woman past the age of 14 is a virgin, and that by the time they graduate from college, your average co-ed will have a "body count" in the hundreds. To add insult to injury these ran through boss babes are scheming to leave their marriages at the 10 year mark so they can "divorce rape" their beta cuck husbands, alienate their children from their fathers and steal half of "his" money and property!

While you should not specifically target the incel as a mark, you should be aware that men of this stripe might be a sizeable percentage of the men who are seeking foreign brides. These men, dissatisfied with their romantic prospects in their home countries, fantasize about finding an ideal wife in a foreign land where they believe women will be more submissive and provide them with the respect they seek.

Ironically, this group is frequently among the most resentful, despite their limited real-world interactions with women. They frequently dismiss advice to "touch grass" and approach women, considering it an exercise in futility. As a result, they often remain virgins well into their 30's and beyond.

Some incels are highly educated but antisocial nerds with well paying jobs in fields such as computer science or engineering. Others are less ambitious—stagnating in their parent's basement, unwilling to make any progress in their lives; this variety of incel overlaps with the hobosexual.

It's worth noting that an incel may undergo a significant transformation in behavior once he experiences the adoration of a woman for the first time. However, there's also a risk that he may seek to punish his partner for past rejections. Due to these complexities, dating an incel can be fraught with risks, and it's prudent to carefully evaluate this prospect throughout the courtship before committing to a relationship.

CHAPTER THIRTY-THREE

THE DIVORCED MAN

We have briefly touched on the mindset of the divorced man and will continue our dissection. The typical divorced man is over 35 years old, and, unlike the incel, has experienced cohabiting in long term relationships.

The divorced man is licking his wounds from the breakdown of his marriage. It is doubtful that he is seeking therapy to see how he contributed to its demise. It is much easier for him to place the blame squarely on the head of his ex, who he believes has been "ruined" by feminism, social media attention and a legal system rigged in women's favor that incentivizes divorce.

More than likely, the recently divorced man will bury his emotions. He may sublimate his grief by turning to drinking, gambling, and partying. Seeking solace in the arms of a new woman, preferably one who will get under the skin of his ex-wife, he will soothe but not heal his bruised ego.

Before the ink is dry on the divorce decree he will rush to create a Tinder/Match/POF account. To his dismay, he discovers that the women in his age range look old and overweight. Never mind that he too, is bald, has a BMI over 30, and has a shriveled manhood. In his mind, he looks good for his age and has retained the same level of attractiveness as he did on his wedding day.

He is disappointed that finding a woman he finds desirable is not a slam dunk. He comes to realize that his age places him outside the preferences of younger women. To compensate, he resorts to lying about his age and posts a picture of himself when he was younger and fitter. He adds an inch or two to his height.

The jig is up once they video call or meet in person, should it progress that far. The divorced man will reach his boiling point. In the best-case scenario, he may have paid for dinners and drinks only to be ghosted afterwards. In a more humiliating situation, the young lady might excuse herself to go to the powder room and then dine and dash, subsequently blocking him on all platforms. Nobody wants an old man.

During this period, his level of frustration is equal to that experienced by incels. He is DONE with women. At least, he says he is. He will voraciously read manosphere bibles to understand female nature. Disgusted by their tomes, he may even join MGTOW (men going their own way), a movement that eschews interaction with women in favor of self-improvement (while simultaneously being unable to stop talking about women).

He is at the end of rope, literally and figuratively. He now understands why male suicides peak in middle age post divorce. He cracks open a beer bottle. Screw his diet. He plops down on the couch and aimlessly scrolls though social media, unfollowing the "instathots" who wouldn't talk to him unless he paid for the privilege through Cash App.

He toggles to one of his favorite manosphere guru's feed. To his astonishment, the don of misogyny has gotten hitched after years of cursing at women's entitlement. Apparently, the cure for male loneliness could be found for the cost of a plane ticket.

CHAPTER THIRTY-FOUR
THE AGING BACHELOR

The aging bachelor wakes up one day in his late 30's or 40's in an existential crisis. He spent his youth partying then sobered up and spent his adulthood at the corporate grind and building his mini empire. It's comprised of a modest townhouse in the suburbs, an SUV, a kayak, perhaps a motorcycle, and a company matched 401k.

His first serious girlfriend in college got tired of waiting for the ring after graduation and moved on to his fraternity brother. Truth be told he never got over that "L", nor did he learn from it. He has wasted more than a few women's prime years in long term relationships that were terminated because he "wasn't ready" to get married or he thought he could get a higher quality babe once he made bank "someday". A man's value goes up as he gets older, or so he was told.

He rubs his eyes. His head is pounding from a massive hangover from the previous night's disappointing festivities.

He turns on the TV which broadcasts a dismal financial forecast. Despite his best efforts at entrepreneurship, he did not become the next Bill Gates. Nor did he become a real estate mogul like Donald Trump. Apart from the apartment building in an undesirable neighborhood he purchased during the last housing crash, he hasn't been able to scale his side hustles as much as he wanted. Creating multiple streams of income was harder than the gumroad courses made it seem.

How will he spend his birthday evening? Not clubbing. Last night was a total disaster. He felt like a "fish" out of water. He didn't recognize any of the music. Everyone was at least 10 years younger than him. None of the girls he attempted to converse with showed any genuine interest beyond him buying them a drink. To add insult to injury, he overheard one of them laughing and referring to him as "gramps" after multiple futile attempts to join their circle. The only things gained (or lost) from the evening were a hangover and a significantly lighter wallet from trying to impress significantly younger women.

When did it become so difficult to pull women? There was a time when it was easy. Well, maybe not easy, but certainly easier. He was never much into one-night stands – but at least he knew he could get one if he aimed for low hanging fruit. Now, the women he found attractive barely looked in his direction. It was depressing.

He scrolls through his phone. It's full of well wishes for his 39th birthday. He is delighted to see happy birthday videos from his nieces and nephews. He loves those kids. He is their favorite uncle.

He laughs ruefully at their "over the hill" jokes. He remembers feeling that way when he was their age—anyone over 30 seemed old.

10 years ago he made fun of his brother (who is better looking and more successful) for getting married when his bucket list wasn't completed. He hadn't traveled around the world, dated a Victoria's Secret model, or jumped out of an airplane. Now, as the aging bachelor rewatches his nephew's antics as he climbs on his father's shoulders, he wonders if his brother had the right idea all along.

He logs into his fake social media account where he is free to express his thirst over instathots and discuss game with manosphere bros. What a load of BS! The bros promised it would be easier to get 10's as he got older. The exact opposite is true! On a whim, he decides to search for his ex-girlfriends. They too have moved on, now happily married with children. Suddenly, the loneliness he had kept at bay for so long caught up with him...

CHAPTER THIRTY-FIVE

THE HOBOSEXUAL

The term "hobosexual" has gained popularity in the national lexicon to describe the orientation of a low status, underachieving male who nevertheless feels entitled to unrestricted pum pum.

The hobosexual has embraced a life of mediocrity. Its members spann various ages from their 20s to their 60s. Their appearance can vary, sometimes appearing younger due to their laid-back lifestyle, while others bear the marks of rough living, having spent their entire minimum-wage earnings on marijuana and Hennessey. When not occupied with jobs at call centers, mall security, or pizza delivery, they can often be found nursing hangovers or indulging in recreational substances. With the passage of time, their ability to recover from all-night benders has dwindled, leaving traces on their faces.

They have shown little inclination for self-improvement, often ending up in menial jobs that require minimal to no skills. This lack of discipline extends to their personal lives and sexual hygiene, leading to multiple instances of unpaid child support owed to different baby mommas.

In their youth, they are given leniency for being broke if they are handsome and charming. The hobosexual who could maintain a façade of working toward a goal or being productive could still pull halfway decent women. Often, they would enroll in community college courses that never resulted in a degree or mastery of a skill, maintaining the illusion of progress.

They might have even finagled a financially supportive partner who saw potential in them. However, the hobosexual failed to capitalize on that opportunity. Over time, their wives or girlfriends grew tired of shouldering the responsibility, hopelessly waiting for the hobosexual to mature and overcome their laziness.

If they don't live with a partner, they might choose to rent a room in a boarding house, share accommodation with roommates, or worst of all, remain in their parents' basement. Unfortunately, some prefer to remain in a state of prolonged adolescence, relying on their parents for meals and laundry without taking on adult responsibilities.

The "Epiphany" phase spares no man, but it can be argued that it wounds the hobosexual the deepest. As the hobosexual ages and "twink death" sets in, he becomes painfully aware of the man's wall. He slams headfirst into the wall that the manosphere falsely promised only existed for women. No longer the cute and boyish ingénue, he discovers that his dusty ways are no longer tolerated by the women he is attracted to, nor the men who's respect he seeks.

Men have two walls: one is financial, and the other is physical. The older a man gets, the more money and status he needs to pull. Conversely, a young and attractive man tends to have a higher desirability, regardless of his income.

No, men do not age like fine wine. The odds of impressing beautiful women dwindle as his hair thins and his muscle mass diminishes. When the ladies he approaches at the club learn the hobosexual only has a seasonal job mowing lawns at his uncle's landscaping company, they immediately bounce, barely suppressing laughter as he laments being laid off during the winter months. Literally the only reason they entertained the old scrote in the first place is to use him for free drinks.

The man's wall is undefeated. An older man (post 30) without resources may as well be a eunuch.

As the manosphere often says, "Facts don't care about your feelings."

The hobosexual can no longer fall back on the excuse of youth to justify his lack of progress in life. He's no longer the youngest guy occupying the lowest rung at work, and management has stopped grooming him for promotions. Mentors have lost faith in him. His father regards him with disappointment, while his mother steadfastly defends him as the baby still clinging to her skirts. Yet, the aging hobosexual can't help but feel a twinge of guilt as his parents argue over his lack of motivation. In private, his mother asks what his future will look like once they are no longer around to care for his basic needs.

It dawns on him that he doesn't know what his future will look like. He is like the grasshopper in Aesop's fable, dependent on others for survival, and utterly unprepared for the inevitable winter.

He has no hope for a legacy. He has neither wife nor children – and quite honestly, no hope of getting one. Communism couldn't happen soon enough. If he could get a fat monthly check from the government, his problems would be solved! Then he could support a family! A state-mandated spouse would be the answer to his prayers.

The hobosexual's real-life circle of friends has dwindled over time. Many of those he attended high school and community college with have moved ahead in life, making it difficult to relate to them. Consequently, he dedicates a significant portion of his time to nurturing online friendships, where he can adopt different personas and escape his reality.

Online, no one can see the empty pizza boxes in his sink and the unkempt bed linens. He opens up his laptop to catch up with the gaming crew on Dischord. To his amazement, his buddy, a gas station attendant on the graveyard shift, announces his engagement. As he shares his intended's profile pic, the gang roasts the groom to be, masking their shock and jealousy that the mid 30's pot-head won over the heart of a babe clearly out of his league!

Where did he meet the lucky lady? Well, they don't make women like that in America…

CHAPTER THIRTY-SIX

PASSPORT BROS

While scouring through Reddit posts to (at worst), fuel their contempt for the modern woman, or (at best), assuage their loneliness, the incel/divorcee/bachelor/hobosexual (heretofore collectively known as "the fish") will stumble upon videos posted by "passport bros".

According to the "sexpats", a treasure trove of traditional wives can be found overseas. Their disciples advocate traveling to poorer, underdeveloped countries, where the US dollar holds significant value. The lower cost of living in these places enables men to lead more opulent lives and impress women with extravagant dates that would be challenging to afford back in the United States.

The third world is populated with thin, beautiful, subservient and women; the antithesis of the American bossbabe. The chaste and modest foreign bride's life mission is to massage her husband's feet after a long day of working and greet him at the door with home cooked meals served with a seductive smile and a negligee in anticipation of dessert. Rather than complain about the division of labor, as their ungrateful American counterpart is wont to do, this fine female specimen takes pleasure in catering to her man's every need. Before he even asks, she will bring a beer to his recliner and cue up his favorite video game.

This is the utopia that awaits the passport bro. His inner stud that lay dormant in the company of masculine, obese American roasties, will suddenly be allowed to blossom in the exotic soil of Thailand, the Ukraine, or Colombia.

Cue the dream sequence.

The Passport Bro is a big baller now. Thanks to the exchange rate, he can check into the finest hotel, which costs the same as a Red Roof Inn back home. He orders room service and gives a generous tip to the bell hop who gushes at the $2USD tip.

He changes into his swim trunks and runs downstairs. The bevy of babes in string bikinis makes his jaw drop. To his shock, two of the gorgeous honeys approach him. This is unprecedented. In the states, being rejected by women he is attracted to and pursues is his default.

He chats with them a while in their adorably broken English, asking where they are from and vice versa. The waiter approaches the new friends. The Passport Bro orders cocktails for himself and the ladies. They all get in the pool and the fine young things giggle at his corny jokes.

All of this happens before he even has the chance to visit the traditional "waifu" (Japanese word for wife that has evolved to mean a trad wife) he met online.

So many choices for the Passport Bro. The newly minted devotee has discovered paradise on earth. Finally he feels SEEN and not ignored. Here are genuine women—women who acknowledge him as the masculine Alpha he has been all along! He is living the life of a Chad.

As the passport bro acolyte sips on his umbrella drink, he reaches under his beach chair and discovers that his wallet is missing. He politely excuses himself and looks everywhere. He enlists the concierge and his new lady friends to help. It's nowhere to be found.

He calls his credit card company. Fortunately, everything except for the cash is replaceable. He chuckles sardonically as he remembers the advice of the Godfather of the Passport Bro movement: always be on the lookout for pickpockets and petty crime. Along with being mugged, drugged, and catfished, it's one of the risks of finding love abroad.

Determined not to allow this hiccup to ruin his vacation, he orders another round for the table. The smiling waiter hands them oversized cocktails. The newly minted friends clink their glasses and toast to good health. The bro in training grimaces.

This one doesn't taste right....

CHAPTER THIRTY-SEVEN
FEMININE VENEER

I'll let you use your imagination to guess what happens next.

This is where the naivete of the Sex-pat will get him into trouble. He is accustomed to residing in a high-trust society, where crime and corruption are relatively rare. Street smarts become essential in second and third world countries, where our protagonist, the simp in training, becomes a prime target.

His Achilles heel is that despite his online diatribes-- above all else-- he craves a woman's love. This insatiable longing, combined with his voracious sexual appetite, clouds his judgment and makes discernment futile. That's why throughout history, some of the most effective spies in every war have been women; the mesmerizing allure of an attractive woman can easily lead even the staunchest alpha wannabes to cast aside their principles.

Geography will never trump female nature. Beneath a facade of femininity, foreign women have honed "game" to acquire creature comforts and financial security -- without their targets being conscious of the subtle entanglement. It's a simple formula—act sweet, submissive and kind until the rings are exchanged.

Our objective is to enchant them before they unravel our intentions. Crafting this fantasy will prove mutually advantageous. By the time they unravel the truth, they will be so enamored and committed that they will love their bondage, Stockholm Syndrome Style!

Happy wife, happy life.

CHAPTER THIRTY-EIGHT

DIVORCED VS INCEL VS BACHELOR VS HOBOSEXUAL

What are the advantages and disadvantages of marrying one of these cohorts over the other?

Incels tend to be younger and have more disposable income. They have neither children nor ex-wives with whom you must share resources.

On the other hand, many incels are on the autistic spectrum, and have a limited ability to feel empathy for others. They can have rigid thinking and behavior and be unwilling to deviate from it.

Many have struggled with untreated depression or other mental illnesses. Seeking solace in porn and OF is how the incel coped with their loneliness. If they refuse to seek therapy, they may express their unhappiness in inappropriate ways, by taking it out on partners.

Unlike the incel, the divorce' has experience with commitment, so he understands compromise and cohabitation in a way that the incel, who has been alone for most of his life, does not.

Many divorced men want to start over and "get it right" the second time around. If they have any introspection about their marriage's demise, they will want to avoid the pitfalls that torpedoed that relationship. If in his first marriage he neglected romance, he may take pains to keep the embers aflame with his new love interest; likewise, he may want to prioritize spending time with children from his second family, if he wasn't an involved father with his older children.

There is a flip side. The divorced man may want you to sign a pre-nuptial agreement. Or he may try to talk you into dating indefinitely, with the argument that marriage is just a piece of paper. He may want to bargain with you, and leave all of his assets to his children, but will pay all of your bills to compensate.

The bachelor has been a serial dater for most of his adult life. He may have been a bit of a player, using pick up artistry to charm women. However, he was most likely involved in multiple yearlong relationships that didn't pan out—due to his own inability to commit and fear of missing out.

Unlike the incel, he doesn't suffer from crippling anxiety and never had a problem getting dates. He doesn't shy away from approaching women online and off. In fact, he enjoys the challenge of "cold-approaching" women in public.

Therefore, it is not uncommon for the bachelor to make the first move and chat you up in person. He can be found in nightclubs, bars, hotel lobbies, socializing and checking out the local talent to see who catches his fancy.

The aging bachelor's clock is ticking loudly in his ear. He will quickly make his move to secure your exclusivity but may get cold feet as he vacillates between the reality of life passing him by and the nostalgia for his Peter Pan existence.

The hobosexual is arguably the least desirable potential target. A certain stripe of hobosexual may have an assembly line of baby mommas with unpaid child support. Your prospects for a long-term future with him are grim unless he is in line to receive an inheritance.

Like all the simps you are considering for marriage, you should hire a private investigator to determine the hobosexual's assets and conduct a thorough background check. You don't want to sleep on an heir, or hitch your wagon to a jail bird.

Most coaches would advise you to treat this specimen like an asbestos waste site. We concur, for the most part. However, this category of male is often the most desperate of all. Their desperation might prove advantageous to you if your other options are not yielding results, and time is of the essence. If properly motivated, he will cobble together a few coins to cover your visa.

CHAPTER THIRTY-NINE

THE EXIT STRATEGY

The hobosexual's American/Canadian/EU citizenship may compensate for his shallow pockets and bleak prospects for career advancement.

You should aim to secure marriage as quickly as possible, followed by obtaining your residency without delay. Regrettably, during the paperwork process, you might have to endure living in his parent's basement or his modest studio apartment. On a positive note, all of this will take place AFTER you have left your home country and established yourself in the US.

Should you go this route, it's advisable to start shopping for your next husband as soon as possible.

Once you are settled in America, seek employment immediately. This won't raise suspicions with the hobosexual husband, as he certainly doesn't earn enough to support both of you. In fact, it may have been one of the things he found refreshing about you, that unlike American women, you didn't care that he dropped out of college and works as a mall security guard. Since he's likely spent his meager savings on importing you to the States and getting your legal status in order, he probably won't object to you entering the workforce shortly after your arrival.

Your choice of workplace is crucial. If you have any office experience, consider applying for an executive secretary position. We recommend this over roles like data entry or customer service because, as a secretary, you'll have direct contact with men in upper management. If you have a trade, such as nursing, seek employment at a hospital in an affluent area.

If you don't have formal education or experience in white-collar fields, don't lose hope. You can apply for positions at exclusive, high-end locations, such as working as a front desk attendant at an upscale gym or a hostess at a fine dining restaurant. When you attend the interview, even if it's for a position like housekeeping, dress professionally, ensure your nails and hair are well-groomed, and communicate clearly in proper English. By presenting yourself well, there's a good chance you can be considered for roles you may not be traditionally qualified for. That's beauty privilege!

Set aside a secret emergency fund of cash. If your husband insists on pooling your finances together, skim off the top and hide it in a safety deposit box or a bank account in a trusted friend or relative's name.

Once you are in the proximity of successful men, it's essential to present yourself well and maintain a cheerful attitude. Though you should be competent at your job, do not appear too perfect. On rare occasions, be slightly late (less than 3 times a year). Your overall demeanor will be upbeat, but it's okay to have days when you seem stressed or a little down, albeit sparingly (perhaps once a week, especially after your probation period) – especially when you know that your male higher ups are watching! Bring the same inexpensive meal for lunch every day.

At some point, you might be asked about your personal life. If it's a female coworker inquiring, you can casually dismiss it, saying everything is fine, and offer a smile. However, if your male boss inquires, it's appropriate to mention that you're juggling work and home responsibilities but express gratitude for the opportunity to learn and work at the company.

As you establish a rapport with your co-workers, you can share some additional, slightly embellished details about your home life. However, always prioritize maintaining an exceptional work ethic. This approach will help protect you from any potential haters who might nitpick at your work performance as a reason to axe you.

If your co-workers inquire about your daily baloney sandwich lunch, you can explain that you're on a tight budget. When they ask about your husband's occupation, you can honestly mention that he works as a car wash attendant and part-time frozen yogurt chef. And if they pry into your living situation, feel free to admit that you reside in your spouse's parents' basement!

If there are any white knights in your office who happen to be attracted to your physical appearance, they will feel compelled to rescue you. They may be among the prospective simps that sit near your cubicle or they may be a middle manager. Once they have figured out that you are unhappy but that THEY can make you laugh and bring a smile to your face, it will give them the green light.

It will begin innocently enough as lunch outings or collaborating on group projects. Slowly drip details about your challenging home life. Your work husband will feel sorry for your indigent circumstances. His starched white shirt will be the shoulder that you cry on. He will feel a strong desire to help you, performing acts of service, leaning into his masculine.

Gradually a workplace romance will blossom. One day, as he is changing your tire in the rain, he will be overcome with passion and kiss you. Allow the moment to happen, but keep it brief, no longer than five seconds. Gently break free and tell him that you care deeply for him, and want to restart your life with him, but you must get a divorce first. You don't want to dishonor each other.

This will serve as a litmus test of his true intentions. If he's serious about your relationship, he will actively search for a lawyer, assist with the retainer fee, and help you find temporary housing.

However, if he hesitates or withdraws, it might indicate he's more interested in an affair. You are not that kind of girl! If he becomes upset, express your intense attraction to him but stress that you must adhere to your moral and religious values. This allows him to save face and walk away. Regrettably, this might require you to begin anew with a different prospect, but that's unlikely if he has stayed by your side for this long.

It is crucial that you refrain from physical intimacy with your new simp and avoid public displays of affection. This will not only build throbbing anticipation for when you both decide to take your relationship to the next level, but it will also keep your reputation intact. Your best course of action is to keep your newfound romance discreet.

At the same time, you will deepen the emotional intimacy. With a feather-light touch on his arm, express how profoundly he has impacted your life; he is the only man who can solve your problems. Share additional details about your unhappy home life, including the fact that you've ceased being intimate with your husband. You never truly loved him in the first place.

Back at the basement, begin discreetly packing your belongings and gradually move them to your new apartment. To avoid suspicion, you can use the excuse of spring cleaning or donating your stuff to create more space in your studio apartment. Given his tendency to spend his free time in a haze of recreational drug use or with his drinking buddies, it's unlikely he'll notice. When you start recognizing the similarities between your spouse's behavior and the dusties from your hometown, you can be assured that you've made the right choice to leave this man-child behind.

It won't be pretty when you break the news of your separation to your husband. The hobosexual husband will suspect infidelity. Deny, deny deny! Be prepared with reasons as to why you are leaving him: his substance use, lack of earning power, and emotional neglect.

You might consider an alternative approach and place the blame on yourself. Explain to him that you're feeling homesick and miss your family, expressing a desire to return to your home country. It's not him, it's you.

He will likely protest and promise to change his ways. He may vow to send you home once a month to see your parents or get a second job. Respond that you love him but you need time to think and request a trial separation. Promptly gather your belongings and leave as soon as possible.

Since neither of you have accumulated many marital assets, there won't be much wrangling over shared possessions. Don't get argumentative about what goes to whom; if it's replaceable, your potential partner will provide it for you. In regard to your soon to be ex-hobosexual, It won't be worth the hassle of squeezing blood from a turnip.

Do your best to keep your new residence a secret and limit your public outings with your new beau. Meanwhile, you'll keep the anticipation high by alternating between being a damsel in distress and a seductress, teasing him about the rewards that await when you are finally free.

Coincidentally, this exit strategy can also be used when leaving the aging bachelor, incel, or divorce'. Never leave your husband without a backup plan and emergency funds. Consult an attorney to make sure that you are in compliance with your visa regulations.

Once the dust of the divorce settles, and you are divested of your dusty, you will be able to "breathe" and start your new life.

As previously mentioned, this path can prove to be burdensome and costly. However, if you find yourself in a situation where you must depart from your home country urgently, it might still be a feasible choice.

CHAPTER FORTY

SYMPATHY FOR THE DEVIL

As much as we tell you to stay detached and not to get your feelings involved, as women, we have a tendency to feel empathy for the less fortunate. Whether that is the homeless, wayward animals, orphaned children, or down on their luck men!

If you have a strong tendency to help the indigent, we suggest you volunteer for a cause that is near and dear to your heart. Reserve those feelings of empathy for charitable organizations, not the men you date.

This is especially true if you decide to marry a hobosexual as a last resort. A poor man, with nothing to lose, can be dangerous.

You see, men base much of their self-worth on their accomplishments. Their accomplishments in turn creates status which earns respect from other men. The caliber of woman on his arm communicates his status non-verbally.

A low status man who doesn't have the respect of other men can be a ticking time bomb. Men that occupy this lowest echelon of society are not only financially broke, but mentally and spiritually broken.

A broke(n) man, who feels powerless in life, will seek to exert power over someone or something that is smaller, weaker and more vulnerable than him. I.E. his woman and his children. His inadequacies will be projected onto his intimate partners and family. Unable to advance in his career and/or amongst his peers, it is likely he will attempt to bully and dominate you, a behavior that may escalate into domestic violence.

It is an unfortunate fact that domestic violence occurs most often in low income households.

Now, we are not saying that your simp is destined to be a wife-beater, but you should be aware that the statistics suggest a correlation between economic status and abuse. Undoubtedly, the inability of a man to provide for his family is a stressor that will create conflict. Financial problems are one of the leading causes of divorce.

We may be preaching to the choir. In your native country, this dynamic is often the norm. Perhaps your parents had this type of marriage, or you are escaping one like this.

Nonetheless, we give you these words of caution, that as humans, we are creatures of habit. If we are unaware of what our unconscious programming is, and do not rewrite that code, we are doomed to repeat it. Do not make the mistake of thinking that your penniless American suitor is any different from the penniless suitors from your village. He suffers from the same proclivities to lash out at his woman in response to his frustrations at his lowly status in life.

Proceed with caution, keep your wits about you. If his behavior changes after marriage, you may have to activate the exit strategy.

CHAPTER FORTY-ONE
WHERE TO CAST YOUR LINE

Now that we've dissected the background and motivations of our simp targets, it's time to roll up our sleeves, grab our fishing rods, and reel in the catch of the day!

It's not just about "going fishing"; we're getting ready for an epic fishing expedition, complete with tall tales about the one that got away (but we reeled back in). We've got our playbook – we know what makes them swim away, what keeps them "up" at night, and what gets them "hooked". Armed with this info, we're not just anglers; we're mind readers!

Where is the best place to drop our lures? The easiest place to cast our lines is online! Thanks to the widespread reach of the internet, we now have access to a larger pool of potential simps than ever before. Gone are the days when women had to mail letters to penpals at a snail's pace, or hanging around shops and taverns near military bases.

Numerous well-known dating platforms cater to simps seeking international connections, drawing lonely hearts from diverse corners of the globe. Within these digital realms, the spectrum of user intentions spans from casual hook ups to the pursuit of serious relationships.

These are few you can check out, although we do not specifically recommend any: International Cupid, Badoo, Bravo Date, Asian Melodies, Single Slavic, Amour Factory and Colombia Lady to name a few. Polyglot is a website where you assess profiles and meet international pen pals, if you want to go under the radar.

Another option is to get Express VPN to mask your location. That way you can get on Tinder or Match and set the location to the countries where you want to find men. You can set it to the US and make connections that way.

If you're a well-educated woman, you've got opportunities to cross paths with interesting simps in a variety of settings. Think about places like language schools, both online and off.

Enroll in classes frequented by businessmen looking to learn your language, and you've got yourself a built-in network where you might discover some romantic prospects.

Exploring the old-school way of meeting in person is still a viable route. Consider service jobs as an option. It's no secret that many a waitress or bartender has stumbled upon love while working in a bustling tourist hotspot. Actor Matt Damon, at the height of his fame, fell in love with and married a single mother who was a bartender at a restaurant he frequented.

The magic ingredient? Well, alcohol often acts as the social lubricant, helping gents shed their inhibitions and flex their flirting muscles. The beauty of it is, unlike the younger American women, you won't label him as a total creep; you'll flash a smile and chuckle at his corny jokes. He'll be pleasantly shocked that you are receptive.

If you have a white-collar gig, you will spend at least 8 hours a day with your American colleagues, which will give you a unique opportunity to assess his work ethic and character. Does he go out for happy hour with the fellas after work or does he go back to his hotel for an early night to recharge for the next day? Does he see this international trip as an opportunity to have no-strings attached sex with the locals and loaf around while his bosses aren't watching, or is he a career focused go-getter? As a coworker you will have a ringside seat to watch him in the professional arena, and then decide if they are worth your time.

CHAPTER FORTY-TWO
HOW TO BAIT THE HOOK

It's safe to assume that most of you will be using online dating platforms to meet your simp. Once you create an account, your next step is to upload your profile. It's very important to craft your profile in a way that will maximize the number of fish you catch. You must bait the hook properly.

Select a body photo that strikes a balance - opt for something modest yet subtly revealing, like donning shorts and a relaxed tank top. Make sure to include at least two photos showcasing your lovely face with natural makeup. Capture yourself in the middle of a fun activity, be it gardening, golfing, or bike riding, allowing your light to shine through. Flash a warm, genuine smile, avoiding an overly staged look. Leave a hint of intrigue; after all, a little mystery can be quite enticing.

Now, let's dive into your bio! Infuse it with a playful, light-hearted, and fun-loving tone that makes your giggle audible through the text. Cast a wide net by setting your target age range from 20 to 60. Even if you're 25! By setting to a wider age range, you will ensnare someone who's willing to spend his surplus money on you. Money that he is unable to spend on young women in his own country who rejected him.

Here is a sample bio that you can modify:

"Hello there! 🌸 I'm a spirited (insert nationality) lady with a zest for life and a heart open to new connections. I've always believed in the beauty of cultural exchange, and I'm here to find an (American/Australian/English) gentleman who shares my love of classic film, golf and bridge. If you're looking for someone to explore life's adventures with let's connect! Age/race unimportant. Can't wait to get to know you better!"

Here is a shorter version:

"Hello! I'm a (insert nationality) woman, filled with a passion for life and a desire to connect with kindred souls. I'm here to find a (American/Australian/English) gentleman who wants to cuddle on the couch and watch sports, take walks on the beach, and go fishing together. Open to all ages/races. Swipe right to share laughter, fun and a homecooked meal!"

These bios make you sound positive, adventurous and open minded. Unlike the bios of American women that he has come across, you do not have a list of criteria that he views as impossibly high.

In his mind, American women's bios look like this:

"I have ridiculously high standards, so you better impress me. If you don't meet my criteria, don't even bother. I'm looking for perfection, and I won't settle for anything less. If you don't like me at my worst, you don't deserve me at my best. You need to be rich, successful, and drop-dead gorgeous. I expect extravagant gifts, constant attention, and you must do everything I say. No short guys, no guys with less than a six-pack, and no one under 6 feet tall. If you can't handle all this, don't waste my time."

No woman's bio looks like this, of course. But he has been rejected so many times he sees Western women as unreasonable, ran-through roasties.

When TWG's craft their bios, they keep prerequisite language out of it.

Even if you are looking for someone who is financially abundant and generous, keep that on the down low. Make it sound as if you are open to friendship with men of all shapes, sizes and ages. This will distinguish you from the American gals he is tired of appeasing.

CHAPTER FORTY-THREE

FEMININITY OUT OF ORDER

There is one way in which the American woman IS traditional. Sure, she will have sex on the third date and give him wifey privileges without a ring—but there is one line she doesn't cross!

Oddly enough, she will not directly ask out or approach a man she is interested in. She may flirt with him, drop hints, or place herself in his orbit—but if he doesn't take the lead she will likely bow out.

When on the date, the woman will do an about face and lean into her masculine, doing all the work. She performs an elaborate mating dance with her accomplishments and education, hoping to impress him. She offers to pay half, if not by the first, then certainly by the third date.

She has ruined what may have developed into the holy grail of marriages by switching into the masculine/pursuer role. From that point onward she is chasing him down – actively seeking (and nagging) to meet him again, suggesting cohabitation, exclusivity, and eventually, dragging him -- kicking and screaming -- to the altar.

The chasing doesn't end. A woman who chases at the beginning will *always* chase—it sets the tone for the entire relationship.

We've heard numerous tales of women who footed the bill for their own engagement rings, weddings, and starter homes in a desperate bid to secure a marriage proposal, only to be unceremoniously cast aside years later for a wounded bird who makes her ex feel like the center of his universe. This new partner might not be as attractive, educated, or witty--but she wasn't present at his lowest moments and therefore views him as his idealized self--a successful, self-made man!

We won't belabor the points we made previously. Suffice to say we will turn this hamster wheel on its axis.

CHAPTER FORTY-FOUR
THE FEMALE NARCOTIC

The strategy of TWG diverges significantly from that of the the western women in a key aspect. TWG will initiate contact but do not actively pursue men, whereas American women refrain from initiating contact but they will pursue once communication is established.

American women will put themselves in the vicinity of men they're interested in, but won't make the first move. However, once a man initiates contact, whether in person or via text/FaceTime, the dynamic shifts and she will quickly catch feelings and start pursuing as he pulls away.

TWG's do the inverse. TWG's will proactively approach if the target fits the criteria, but never chase. This will perplex her potential simps and if he finds her attractive, compel him to pursue.

This contrasts most dating coaches' advice which discourages women from making eye contact or showing overt interest. In specifically targeting foreign men, particularly ones that may not have been very successful with the opposite sex and who may live thousands of miles away, TWG's adopt a different tactic. TWG will nuke our targets with a taste of our feminine love narcotic, then remove it from under their noses.

Incidentally, this approach is not dissimilar from the "love bombing" tactics that narcissistic men use to quickly seduce women into bed and make them desperate for their validation. However, we TWG's will not be giving up the pum-pum until marriage.

(It's quite bold, but one of our students reeled in a whale by wearing a harlequin mask and planting a brief kiss on his lips before she was whisked away in a nightclub crowd. He spent the next 3 days searching for her like Prince Charming with Cinderella's slipper. They are married today.)

If you are on an app that allows you to message men, do not hesitate to message them FIRST. Although you may not need to message anyone first, as you will undoubtedly be inundated with DM's within an hour of setting up your profile. Nonetheless, devote some effort into weeding through profiles and swiping right on the ones that look promising.

Your simps-to-be will be delighted to make your acquaintance. Dating has been a disaster for them and meeting a gorgeous woman who doesn't reject them outright for being dorky/old/overweight will be like a breath of fresh air. You will be sweet, fun, and bubbly. You will apply no pressure for them to perform. This will immediately draw them in. For once they don't have to humiliate themselves by being a "try-hard".

You will be perched on the edge of your seat, fully engrossed in their life stories without interrupting them. Be fascinated by their tall tales of triumphs and trophies. If they complain about work, remind them of their past successes, and how they succeeded against all odds. Show you are an attentive listener by repeating the story back to them of the time they lead the team to the highest sales quarter. Only they, with their unique skill sets, can solve these complex problems.

Even though you are separated by continents, you will be their biggest cheerleader, rooting for them from afar.

Before long, he finds himself addicted. He *feels* good every time you talk. The way you make him feel eclipses any shortcomings you might have—even the ones he claims are deal breakers. In your presence he feels like he can slay any dragon. He feels worthy and attractive for the first time in a very long time, or maybe for the first time ever.

Your sweetness will be chased with salt. Switch up the routine. Without any warning, retract your warmth and light. If they are used to your nightly calls at 7pm, postpone/cancel at the last minute.

Never be too predictable. Never be too perfect.

Imperfections give Erections!

Don't believe it? Look at the infamous cases of beautiful models whose marriages ended in infidelity and divorce, even if, on the surface, the ladies were perfect "10's". Adriana Lima is a prime example. She was a beautiful and devout Catholic who preserved her virginity for marriage, yet being a runway model adored by millions did not exempt her from the cardinal rule : be anything but predictable!

Now, our simps do not necessarily equal the caliber of the high value men who marry supermodels (Our simps may be better specimens, in fact). However, there is a lesson there—being the perfect wife on paper does not guarantee that the relationship will have longevity.

Girls who are thoroughly good are thoroughly boring (even though men claim otherwise). You are capable of being bad – and this excites your simp.

You do not need to look like Giselle to tame your simp. Find your niche. Be *HIS* type.

Thanks to men's fetishes, rest assured that there is a man out there who is guaranteed to be attracted to you. Consider the reality show "600 pound life"—none of the bedridden women are single. They are all catered to by their devoted simps who feed, bathe, and love them, despite (or perhaps because of) their massive size.

Or take the famous example of French President Macron, who is happily married to a woman who is 24 years his senior. His wife, Brigitte, thought he would fall in love with a girl his own age, yet he was steadfastly devoted to her. Today, their public appearances, proudly holding hands, defies conventional expectations for what a high value marriage should look like.

Similarly, Marcus Lemonis, known for his success in business and in television, has a significant age gap with his partner. His wife Bobbi is 25 years older than him, and makes no effort to appear younger, proudly wearing her lined visage. Marcus (like Macron), despite having the means and status that could have afforded him a wide range of choices in partners, found a deep and meaningful connection with Bobbi. This union brought no tangible benefit to Marcus, as Bobbi has neither the wealth nor status to match his. The heart wants what the heart wants.

This is not to say that you should not put effort into looking and feeling your best. However, do not despair if you do not fit into the ideal height, weight, or age bracket. There is a lid for every pot.

What is most important, after you pass *HIS* personal barometer of physical attraction, are the feelings you stir inside of him. You are the alchemist, who turns his lead heart into gold bullion.

You, his dream girl made flesh, will dispense regular hits of your loving presence, then pull back when he least expects it. Reappear and be very sweet, loving, and fun, as if nothing ever happened. It will make him addicted to your feminine narcotic.

CHAPTER FORTY-FIVE

THE ROSTER

Another mistake American gals make is to give exclusivity to men when it is not reciprocated. An American woman will date until she finds a guy she can envision herself settling with. Perhaps he has a decent, middle-class job, is a high tier normie in terms of looks, and isn't a party animal. Thus, she sees his potential as a husband and father of her future children.

Even if he hasn't said a peep about claiming her, she will stop dating others and focus on this man. This will lead to her anxiously attaching to him, walking on eggshells to not offend him, proving her worth, while desperately hoping their tete a tetes will lead to marriage one day.

You will do the opposite. Even though you are throwing love grenades, you will continue to date multiple men, allow them to court you *simultaneously*. You will cull them only if they balk at providing. The "keepers" will prove themselves by giving you gifts, paying your bills, and expeditiously planning your engagement and marriage. From this roster of simps you will choose.

Until then, diversify. Chat with multiple men. We suggest keeping a notebook or a spreadsheet so that you can notate their likes/dislikes, their quirks, their geographic locations, age, screen name, where you met them, and their back stories.

This is important because you don't want to alert your simps in waiting to the fact that they are not the only "fish in the sea"! Note that once a man takes interest in you, he will want you to be exclusive to him, even if he is not exclusive to you yet! So you should keep a low profile once he has made a financial contribution to your maintenance. His financial investment unlocks the door to your love and fidelity.

Remember to keep your stories straight. There is nothing more embarrassing than mixing up a name and a story. You will have to think on your feet to save face after that faux pas. Better to be prepared with your detailed log of each fish in your tank.

You are human. If you do happen to slip up despite taking precautions not to mix up your simpfolk, GASLIGHT him. Deny you said anything incriminating. Accuse him of being too sensitive. Look at him as if he has grown another head. Blame the poor internet connection or the language barrier for his misunderstandings. Your pidgin English clearly confused him. If all else fails, cry, because he doesn't trust you and believe in your love.

As we said earlier, we must think of dating as a business. Take it seriously and devote the time and energy to keep your ledgers balanced. The balance statement of your relationships should show a net profit on your beauty and charm investment.

Remember, TWG's do not put all their eggs in one basket! Until he pays up and the wedding date is set within 6 months, you are SINGLE!

CHAPTER FORTY-SIX

ON WEALTHY MEN

There exists one notable exception to the American woman's rule of not making the first move. If the man is wealthy (by first world standards), and/or famous with the status to match, the rules go out the window. The catch will morph into a whale, compelling women to cast aside any shyness to bag a multimillionaire celeb or magnate.

Keep in mind that these wealthy men have an abundance of options. They are not thirsty whales. Women throw themselves at them all the time, often without commitment on the table. These titans of industry do not publish screeds on incel forums about how awful modern women are, because they have access to the cream of the crop.

We are not saying that it is impossible for you to snag a handsome, wealthy and successful man. It is simply that you will be competing with the American women in their backyard. These men, unlike the incel, divorced man, bachelor, or hobosexual, have not experienced scarcity in the dating marketplace.

If you do happen to encounter a whale, pretend you don't know who he is. Be pleasant but do not give him any special treatment. He is already used to being fawned over. That you are unaware of his identity and treat him as a civilian may appeal to him.

Do not fumble the bag by skipping the 90 day rule and jumping into bed right away. His wealth is not the key to unlocking your legs during the courtship phase.

As you do with your other simps, you will use your conservative upbringing as the reason why you cannot be intimate with him. If he has fallen for you, this will not put him off. Rumor has it that George Clooney, the most famous eligible bachelor, respected his future wife's conservative middle eastern upbringing and did not pressure her for sex prior to their marriage.

You will not allow intimacy until marriage, or at the very least, after the engagement date (and ring) has been set. By this time, you will have accumulated thousands of dollars in gifts and experiences, so even if the engagement ends, you will still come out ahead.

Some of our readers may balk at calling a billionaire a simp. You must remember that no matter how rich he is, the simp gene will be activated in the presence of his queen. Observe Jeff Bezos, who is madly in love with a "post-wall" single mother; she is the spokesperson for his philanthropic organizations and his companion as they jet set from St. Barts to Basel and Miami. He is never happier than when he can be of service and please his lady love.

If your feminine narcotic appeals to the billionaire simp, nothing will stop him from claiming and simping for you.

CHAPTER FORTY-SEVEN
TWO TIMING TIME WASTERS

TWG's are strategic. It's crucial to use discernment to filter out the time wasters.

Not all the men sliding into your DM's have noble intentions of finding love and companionship, let alone a wife. They may be married/in an LTR (long-term relationship), limbo dancers, or too poor to buy a plane ticket.

Why do men waste our time like this? Some chat online for the ego boost of having a curvaceous cutie at rapt attention who provides an emotional tampon for their "woe is me" stories.

It is a sad commentary on the state of modern relationships. The absence of simping has depleted the romance in 50/50 marriages/relationships. Time-wasting husbands are ignorant of the fact that simping will be of mutual benefit to himself and his wife.

Tragically, the man with the wandering eye believes that the reason the fire in his loins has extinguished is because of something his wife has failed to do, when in fact it's because he either stopped simping or never simped in the first place. To add insult to injury he will express that compulsion to simp to strangers on the internet, rather than their spouses lying next to them! If when/their wives ever find out, they are shocked that their husbands, who forgets their anniversary, is writing love sonnets to women they've never met.

The American wives/girlfriends are confused as to why their men would look elsewhere, when they have done somersaults to deliver EXACTLY what men demanded--a female roommate who goes halfsies on the household expenses and maid service to boot.

That, said, whether they are caught by their partners or not, the mental gymnastics that men perform to wiggle out of personal responsibility is impressive. Those involved in emotional affairs never meet their online pen pals in person, so in their minds, they did not cross the line into cheating.

For these fellas, building intimacy over messenger is enough to feed their appetite for a woman's validation. They don't need to EVER see you in real life. Your written declaration of love gives them sustenance. Even your disappointment and anger when they cancel plans to fly out to your country satisfies them because they know they have the power to make you FEEL. It's a woman's indifference that terrifies them!

So, how do you avoid these time wasters? Firstly, avoid any man who refuses to show you his face. There is a good chance he is either attached, poor and/or a catfish.

If he does show his face and chats with you, be mindful of when he speaks to you. Can he only speak during certain times of the day? Is his phone turned off after business hours? Does he never answer calls —but calls you back in hushed tones hours later? If so, there is a good possibility he may be stepping out on his marriage, while he steps outside to talk to you.

Obviously, steer clear of men who are cheap. A man who cares will gift you something, even as simple as a decent headset so you can communicate clearly. If he avoids buying you anything, it means he is either cheap, poor, or afraid of his wife questioning his credit card statement. If he makes excuses, it's NEXT!

It's not uncommon for men to fall in love at first sight. A besotted simp will fly out to meet you sooner than later, often within a month or so of meeting. If more than 4 months go by (6 months at most) without him visiting you, question his intentions.

You, as the woman, should be riding the brakes and pacing the relationship, not him. If he repeatedly pushes back the meet up, it is a sign that he may be hiding something. Even a man with a corporate 9-5 job has at least two weeks of vacation. If those two weeks are already accounted for, he may be taking his family on a vacation, not you.

For the time waster, it is the thrill of the chase, and not the physical contact that makes them feel alive. The satisfaction that he has conquered your heart is enough. If, at any point, he feels pressured to arrange a meeting, he may abruptly cancel, delete his profile, or block you.

Yet another type of time waster is the scrote who seeks a perpetual long term relationship without marriage. He may not be a skirt chaser. In fact, he may be perfectly faithful. However, he comes up with one excuse after another to postpone marriage indefinitely. One of his favorite excuses is citing the wallet depleting child support from his previous marriage—conveniently giving him at least 18 years to stall. This risk-averse fellow wants all of the advantages of marriage (his mate's fidelity, companionship, and maid services) while evading the legal and financial responsibilities it entails. By keeping the relationship off paper, the woman he supposedly loves with be left with nothing if he dies suddenly or decides to skip town after 10 years. Scrooge doesn't love his pretend wife, he loves the convenience.

We will say it again: avoid married men. Some coaches, while not explicitly endorsing it, cite mitigating circumstances as a reason to overlook a man's marital status. They argue that his marriage might be on the brink of collapse, and his growing attraction to you could be the catalyst for him divorce. Furthermore, if the simp is relatively well-off, it may take time to sort his finances and hammer out a divorce settlement.

Nonetheless, we do not endorse this approach. Our objections aren't solely based on moral considerations. A married man may intentionally pursue women on the international dating sites to avoid being discovered by his wife. The geographical separation diminishes the urgency to arrange in-person meetings, enabling him to keep his pen pals in a state of limbo indefinitely.

Even if a man is single when you meet him, there is a good chance he will encounter resistance to your relationship from his family and friends back home. They will have heard the horror stories about foreign brides being unrepentant gold diggers (true) who will marry anyone with a pulse to escape to America (somewhat true). Your simp will need fortitude and a foggy pair of love goggles to endure the objections to your union.

A married simp adds a layer of struggles to your life you don't need--when your objective is to secure a life of ease!

If you choose this path, your reputation will be in tatters. You will be viewed as a home wrecking ho' who is trying to destroy his family. There is a good chance he will go back to his wife if caught and you will have wasted time when you could have been courted by an eligible man.

If this time waster is kicked out of his house by his wife and lands on your doorstep, it will be under duress and not because it's his earnest desire. If you do give the relationship a go, you will have to live with the stigma of infidelity and wait for it to die down, if ever. His children will loathe the sight of you and cockblock the re-marriage pipeline. That's after you wait years for his divorce to be finalized.

For all these reasons, we do not advocate dating married men. For the majority of women, it does not have a happy ending.

However, we do not give prescriptions. We understand that for some, the sweet nectar of a wealthy man's wallet is irresistible. If you do go this route, be prepared for the fallout when infidelity is discovered and a lengthy waiting period as the separation prior to divorce ensues. Once the ink is dry, Prince Charming may not be in a hurry to get committed again and suddenly decide they want to play the field, leaving you in limbo.

In our opinion, it is not worth the headache when there are so many lonely single men in the world. It would be easier to choose from among the free men than to wait for the married man to become free.

TWG don't waste time.

CHAPTER FORTY-EIGHT
THE FUTURE FAKER

Future faking is common with married bottom feeders but can also lurk amongst different varieties of simps.

Talk is cheap. Future faking is a common tactic to lull you into a false sense of emotional intimacy. When a FF (future faker) paints a vivid picture of a shared future, a naïve woman will open her heart (and her legs) based on empty promises.

The modus operandi of a FF goes like this: he will match with a lady who excites him physically on the app. They will embark on a fast and furious texting relationship. The man will cite his busy work schedule for his inability to arrange a date right away. Therefore, he will "court" her over text and facetime with his honeyed words.

In the morning, she will wake up to a "good morning beautiful" text from her dating app match. Throughout the day, he will pepper her with questions, acting genuinely interested in her hopes and dreams. He will share details about his life, what he is looking for in a life partner (which happens to coincide with what she wants) and wonder out loud how well they will mesh in person when they get along so swimmingly online. He will be flirtatious, but if he's a pro, he won't go heavy on the sexual innuendo—he knows that will turn most women off at the beginning. Before she goes to bed, her phone will ding with a "good night gorgeous" text.

After a few weeks passes and the tension has reached a fever pitch, he will make a date to meet in person. If married or in a long-term relationship (LTR), he will suddenly cancel the date or simply delete his account. This variety was in it for the validation and ego stroke. He wanted to know that he still "had it" and could attract women. Once he is satisfied that he made his lady love fall for him, he will terminate things abruptly.

The second variety of future faker will follow through with the date, usually 2 weeks to a month or so after initially matching. By this time, the woman will feel like she already knows this man, even though they have never met. They have been speaking on the phone every morning while she drives to work, and in the evening, after she brushes her teeth and gets ready for bed. They have been texting non-stop, for hours throughout the day.

It feels like she has been gallantly courted, but in truth all she had was an online pen pal. The phone marathons mimic commitment. When he walks in the door and meets her at a restaurant or bar, it will be the culmination of weeks of anticipation. This is when he will shmooze her and tell her how she is the woman he has been waiting for his entire life. She is even more beautiful in person than in her profile.

He will dress sharply, smell good, and drive a high end car. While he will mostly act interested in her life, he will slip in suggestions that they go to an upscale art auction or shopping for a new luxury car.

The Future Faker will escalate to get physical right away. It will feel like the next natural step after they have forged what she thinks is a deep connection from the hours they spent on the phone. He has prepped her for it!

If he isn't successful at getting her into the sack on the first physical date, the love bombing will continue. He will make plans for the future, asking her where she wants to raise her children and what does she think of private school? Making grandiose plans takes the place of truly getting to know each other.

The American girl will fall in love with "the plan". She will be addicted before she knows who he really is.

Once she falls into bed with the Future Faker, the mask slips off. This is when the abuse and neglect starts. Ironically, this will be when it is most difficult to leave the narcissist/future faker. He will intermittently leave bread crumbs of his former kind and loving gestures to make her think the utopia they planned together is just around the corner.

The sexual connection between the future faker/narc and his partner (also known as his supply) will be the most intense she has ever known. The reason why is because intimacy is the only way to feel connected to the FF after he has ghosted, triangulated (pitting her against a rival for his affections), and gaslit her.

Months or years may pass by as women wait for their beloved to morph back into the person they pretended to be in the beginning.

As a TWG, you see the folly of this modern dating disaster. It is a situation that could have been avoided with a jaundiced eye toward grandiose gestures and empty promises. Put up or shut up.

This is a challenge that long distance relationships must be on the lookout for. Long distance time wasters can keep up their ruse for a longer period of time. It is quite easy for a time waster to cultivate an emotional affair with a woman who is thousands of miles away. Due to the distance, he has a perfect excuse for why he can't meet within a week of matching.

The simplest way to screen for time wasters is to create a scenario where he could solve an issue by buying you something. As you build a rapport, let him know that you have a cheap headset and it's hard to communicate. If he volunteers to buy you a new one and ships it to you immediately, he passes the first test. If he's willing to buy you things, he has made an investment, however small, in you. This will segueway into paying for other expenses and gifts.

On the other hand, a FF will back off despite having bragged about his net worth, his homes, boats, and cars. All of a sudden he will claim he is in the middle of a legal dispute and his accounts are frozen! So, unfortunately, all of the jewelry and purses he planned on buying you will be put on hold.

Laugh to yourself and make mental note of this red flag. Back off from your interactions and react to his frozen accounts with a lukewarm shoulder. See if he rushes to fill in the void with all of the gifts he initially promised. If not, gradually next him if he doesn't prove his love materially.

He may come through with gifts and money but put off seeing you in person. This can be a thorny situation as you can quickly become a "sugar" addict. If your end goal is marriage and emigration, you should evaluate if this is serving you. Keep this prospect around right up until you are married (to another person). You can keep this one around for your benefit but be careful that you do not focus on him to exclusion of others because of the shiny trinkets and baubles you are given.

The next breed of FF is the married man, who we have already discussed. This one will either totally avoid meeting you, or he will meet you at regular intervals when his work takes him traveling. In fact, you may have met him on one of his business trips. You can sniff him out by observing his spending habits. He will pay cash and refuse to use his credit card, even though it has consumer protections. This is because he doesn't want a paper trail to be discovered by his wife.

The married FF will have you thinking that you have a future together because he sees you and spends money on you. This, however, rarely ends well. More than likely, he will not leave his wife and continue to have his cake and eat it too.

The last type of FF is the hobosexual/poorcel. Even if he has fallen for you, hook, line, and sinker, he doesn't have the funds to make it happen. It's possible he might pool together his meager resources to buy you a gift, but it is doubtful that he will be able to so do on his call center salary. He will likely fail the headset test, so you can cut his head off early.

Remember, a man of means is only valuable if he shares the loot with you. Believe it or not, there are dusties in the wild who are tight fisted with women but enjoy the attention and clout they receive with extravagant displays of wealth. Do not be swayed by his luxury vehicle, swiss watch, and designer suit. Unless he purchases you a wardrobe, jewelry and car to match, it's all a future faking ruse designed to give him a shortcut to your body.

CHAPTER FORTY-NINE

ON MALE GAME

Upon request we are including a brief chapter expanding on male game. By holding fast to our TWG standards, we are anesthetized against PUA (pick up artist) tricks and traps. The wannabe PUA's success hinges on getting us emotionally hooked by rushing into intimacy. As we stated previously, this is accomplished by future faking and love bombing.

Obviously, we will not allow ourselves to jump into bed quickly. This is reserved for after the $10,000 rule has been satisfied and the rings are exchanged (or at least engagement for American women). However, there is another trick that PUA's use to try to circumvent the cardinal rule of never chasing men.

We refer to this as the diminishing returns game. Initially, he devotes 100% of his time to his new love interest, engaging in hours long phone conversations, sending good morning and good night texts, and surprising her with flowers and candy. This pattern continues for a while until, seemingly out of nowhere, he reduces his attention by 5%. Perhaps he skips the morning text, leaving the woman puzzled but silent. His next step is to further decrease his effort by another 5%, omitting the good night text. At this point, his effort level is at 90%, causing the woman to grow uneasy but hesitant to voice her concerns.

The cycle continues as he gradually decreases his efforts, forgetting dates and skipping romantic gestures, until he reaches a mere 20% effort. At this stage, any slight increase in effort, even just

10%, feels significant to her, as she has grown accustomed to accepting the bare minimum, hoping that someday he will return to giving his all.

She will finally gather the courage to ask why he has grown so distant and unavailable. He will respond with every excuse in the book: "I've been so busy with work, babe" or "I've been dealing with a lot of stress." In truth, this is a trick designed to induce panic in women, making her fear that she is losing his interest and affections, triggering her to chase and "win" him back.

This tactic has grown so prevalent that dating advice sites are inundated with women asking how to rekindle their relationships and men's coaching groups boasting testimonials on its success.

You may think you are immune to such manipulation, but surprisingly, some of our friends have succumbed to it, prompting us to delve deeper. Typically, the TWG will falls prey to this if the man has heavily invested in the beginning stages. Suddenly, the money and lavish gifts stop when he claims to have fallen on hard times and lost his source of income. He reassures her that the financial difficulties are temporary and diligently applies for jobs while future faking her with promises of vacations they will go on and properties they will buy when he is back on his feet. When he finds employment, he continues to be tight-fisted with gifts, saying he needs to tighten his belt temporarily.

For this reason, we reiterate our advice to keep a roster. This scenario underscores the need to screen for hidden stinginess of heart and wallet in the courtship phase. Do not be swayed by promises of a pay off when he makes the big sale or when he receives a settlement check. Consider him it only if he has spent lavishly in the past. If it continues, be prepared to walk, and follow through.

Meanwhile continue dating others and avoid pinning your hopes on a simp's potential. This is where the positive "intangibles"—such as a gentle demeanor, sense of humor, and physical spark have a danger of clouding your judgment when he backpedals on the elaborate dance he performed to win you over. This is why dating multiple men is so important-- it serves as a safeguard against becoming overly invested and keeps you grounded in reality.

CHAPTER FIFTY

THE RIGHT TO CHOOSE

Once you have successfully executed these strategies, you will have a buffet of simps to choose from. How to decide which simp will win your hand?

Before you decide who you will marry, remember this. Your lifestyle and status will rise or fall to the level of your husband's. If you marry a blue-collar cable guy, your life will one of limited means. Once he is back on American soil and the exchange rate is no longer is in favor, his extravagant spending will cease and he'll be back to fishing for change in his greasy overalls to pay for gas. Say goodbye to the fine dining and 5 star hotels you enjoyed together in your home country. On the other hand, marrying an upper middle class man will give you a 3 bedroom house in the suburbs and a yearly vacation or two.

Divorce is always an option once you get your papers, but, we acknowledge that a female's soft heart is a pernicious thing. Sometimes love blooms even when do our best not to water it.

Therefore, it is always best to keep our wits about us and think logically and with foresight. Like a businessman, make decisions based on the balance sheet, not on your emotions, which are fleeting.

This advice applies to our American audience as well. Though you can certainly outearn your spouse, he will resent your success. You may feel guilted into making yourself "small" to appease his ego. As a result of your choices, you may have to live in a less than desirable neighborhood, send your children to subpar public schools, and scrimp and pinch for a road trip vacation. It's in your best interests to keep the lifestyle you will have with your future husband at the forefront of your mind before choosing to be in love with him.

Make no mistake, love is a choice. If you choose to love and honor a brokie, it will effect the entire trajectory of your life and your children's lives.

The honeymoon phase fades fast. The initial excitement of a new relationship will eventually give way to the reality of everyday life with your chosen partner.

Be wise. Be prudent. Choose wisely.

CHAPTER FIFTY-ONE
CHARACTER COUNTS

It may appear that we are shallowly focused on a man's finances and perceived worthiness as a simp when considering him as a potential husband.

But should we not also value qualities like the ability to open jars, a good sense of humor, car repair skills, a square jawline, tall height to reach high shelves, and muscular arms capable of defending you in dangerous situations?

Indeed they do matter. However, they rank lower on the priority list than bank balances and simp status. Once the criteria for finances and simp compatibility have been met, then you are free to screen for body fat percentages or dimpled chins.

We understand your desire to bear beautiful children. We really do. But your decision to make him your simp baby daddy must not hinge on his chiseled features. If he brings enough shekels to the table you will barely see his weak chin in the dim lighting of the 5 star restaurants you frequent because he loves spoiling you.

What about niceness, you may ask? The way you test if a man is truly nice or not is how he reacts when he doesn't get what he wants. If you say "no" to him, and he erupts into a rage or ghosts, then you will know that he isn't very nice after all. For this "nice guy", acting nice is a means to an end.

What about a kind, calming and gentle demeanor? Say the simp you are leaning towards demonstrates skill at conflict resolution, never raises his voice and always remembers birthdays and anniversaries. Shouldn't that count for something? It certainly does.

We say that once your material needs are met, and consideration for your likes and dislikes are prioritized, 99% of problems in relationships are solved. It's said that financial problems are the number one leading cause of divorce.

No matter how sweet and conscientious he seems in the courtship phase, his true character will emerge if money problems arise. If there isn't enough money to pay rent or keep the utilities on, you will see the shadow side of his personality he takes pains to hide when in the throes of love.

The way a man handles his finances reveals his character. It demonstrates how his discipline and problem solving abilities. The time and effort he has put in to learning markets dynamics, leveraging debt, using credit wisely, and actively growing his portfolio. True provision is taking calculated risks but also faithfully socking away money every month for retirement and his future children's college funds—not playing video games and complaining about capitalism.

Living worry free about the basic necessities of life will give you peace of mind that transcends all understanding. Not having to stress about the electricity being shut off or having your car repossessed will allow you to focus on keeping fit, monetizing on your side hustles, and parenting your children.

We have heard from many women who ask if they should date men who make substantially less income than they do, lack education and ambition to improve their lot in life. They want to know if they should make an exception to the $10,000 rule because their simp makes sure to fill their gas tank, changes their oil, and serves them breakfast in bed.

We do not suggest that the American woman take this route. Studies have shown that a woman outearning her husband has a greater likelihood of divorce. Furthermore, it is very likely that a woman will not be mentally stimulated if her husband is less accomplished than she is, leading to "dead bedroom" as the manosphere calls it. Love will not pay the bills. The long term implications of marrying down must not be swept under the rug because of a ticking biological clock.

How he takes care of you *IS* his character. Remember, if he does not tap into his natural submissiveness and desire to be led by providing, he will never be happy. And he will project his unhappiness unto you.

TWG should only consider low earners if they can muster up the funds to pay for their visa. Once they reach American soil they should reassess and see if the relationship is worth salvaging or if they should trigger the exit strategy.

CHAPTER FIFTY-TWO

MOVE IN SILENCE

We hear so much about men's game. They make no bones about their shortcuts to getting women into bed as quickly and with as little investment as possible.

What is woman's game? It is how women survived in a world where men are physically bigger and stronger and controlled the laws. Yet she *persisted*—and got the bag. She won by keeping her thoughts, opinions and goals to herself.

Whereas a man crows about his accomplishments (real or imagined), a woman moves in silence.

TWG are discreet. Once you embark upon this lifestyle, it is best for you to keep your ambitions to yourself. Do not to give an audience to the naysayers who tell you it will never work. In fact, they are telling on themselves about what they were never able to accomplish! Avoid the headache by not telling them your plans in the first place.

Do not post excessively on social media, particularly when sharing snapshots of your lavish dates. Excessive displays may inspire jealousy in your simps and your friends. A pinch of jealousy bakes the cake but a pound will burn it. You can post fun activities with your family but take care to avoid looking overly extravagant. Do not pose with a luxury car and a rent-a-babe as the RP gurus do. You can be a gold digger at heart but project a more balanced and grounded image publicly.

Exercise caution in your online interactions, especially when it comes to engaging with content from 'level up' or gold-digging groups.

It's important to ensure that your social media activity doesn't reflect a negative or hostile attitude towards men. Avoid liking or commenting on misandrist posts (even if that's what he does for misogynistic content!). Strive to maintain a positive and respectful online presence.

CHAPTER FIFTY-THREE

THE VISIT

Your international courtship is progressing well. Whether you've connected online or in person, you've certainly captured his interest. He makes the effort to write or call you every day, demonstrating his keenness to keeping the connection strong across the distance.

Initially, your relationship will likely be long-distance, with your dates taking place over Zoom calls. During these virtual meetings, maintain a light and playful demeanor. Laugh, flirt, and smile to keep the atmosphere fun. Occasionally, you can present a small challenge that allows your suitor to offer assistance, showcasing his helpfulness and skills. For instance, you might mention that your younger brother is struggling with his college application essay. This opens an opportunity for your simp to offer his expertise in editing for clarity and grammar, contributing to your brother's education. Such interactions benefits your family and strengthens your connection through the act of service.

While it's important to be engaging and present during your dates, maintaining a balance in your availability is key to preserving an air of femininity and mystery. Focus fully on the moment when you're together, but outside of these times, be a bit elusive. Vary your response times to messages; sometimes reply promptly, and other times, allow a few hours before responding. This approach keeps your interactions dynamic and prevents predictability. Mixing things up in this way can keep the interest alive in your long-distance courtship.

If he complains that you aren't available enough for him, explain that you need to work to support yourself and your family. You would love to be there for him, but unfortunately you need to make a living. If this triggers his protective and provider instincts, he may be the right simp for your purposes. If he does not, it's time to move him all the way down the roster, and out the door if he doesn't step up and prove his love financially.

As part of your dating strategy, you'll spin plates to determine who best aligns with your goals. This approach naturally limits the amount of time you can focus on any one individual. While this is an integral part of the vetting process, you will not disclose this detail to him. Dating multiple people concurrently allows you to maintain a level of detachment, enabling you to assess your simps more objectively. This balanced perspective is key in making informed decisions about your romantic life.

Should he express concern about your availability, you can explain that your work commitments and family responsibilities require significant attention. Emphasize that while you value your time with him, your livelihood and supporting your family are priorities. This response not only sets healthy boundaries but also provides an opportunity to gauge his reaction. If this triggers his protective instincts and a willingness to support you, this could indicate that he is a keeper. However, if he fails to contribute positively to your bottom line, it's time to move him all the way down the roster, and out the door if he doesn't step up and prove his love financially.

Exercise caution if he attempts to steer the conversation to sexual topics. We do not recommend allowing yourself to be coerced into webcamming with him. Some women have had success in wrangling a simp this way, but in our opinion, the risks outweigh the rewards. There is a possibility he might be recording the spicy exchange. If that happens, any risque' footage could be shared without your consent. We think an occasional low cut top or snug sweater is enough to allow him to use his imagination for spank material later, when he fantasizes about seeing you in the flesh.

You can be a little suggestive but remember that less is more. If he pressures you for phone sex gently remind him that you come from a conservative culture. Let him know that while you share his excitement and anticipation, your values and traditions guide you to express such desires only within the bounds of marriage.

Soon enough, his eagerness to meet you in person will lead him to book a flight. When you see him in person, look as beautiful as possible. Allow him to hug and kiss you, but don't let him get too handsy; having your parents or friends there to chaperone will break his passionate momentum. Break off the embrace slightly before he does.

When you are in his presence, be the woman of his dreams. Be focused on him. Mostly. Once in a while, excuse yourself to use your phone. When he asks who it is, say it is your parents, or a work matter. This subtle action arouses his curiosity and a hint of competitive anxiety, making him wonder about your other interactions. However, moderation is key. Don't overdo it. He wants to feel like he is the man you chose, and he is the best (and only) one of the bunch.

Speaking of work...while on one of your dates, let him know that you need to cut the date short due to work commitments. You could also have a friend call, pretend to be your boss, and say that they need you to come in on your day off to take over the shift. Your date will be disappointed. However, inform him that because of your expenses, you are unable to refuse work requests. This approach provides an opportunity for your partner to demonstrate support by offering to cover your lost wages to extend your time together.

This strategy establishes a significant precedent, positioning him in the role of a provider. Express genuine gratitude and affection for his financial support. Your appreciative and warm response will deeply resonate with him, strengthening the bond between you.

Anticipate the possibility of a marriage proposal at the conclusion of his visit. He might even seek a private conversation with your parents to formally request your hand in marriage. This is a tradition that he would never respect in America, as his dating life prior to landing on your shores was anything but traditional. But the magical exotic soil of his beloved's homeland has inspired him to grand romantic gestures like this.

You will want to prep your parents for the proposal. When your simp voices his intentions, they should listen quietly. With a stoic expression, they will explain that in their culture, a groom to be will gift the bride's family with a dowry. Your fella may be slightly taken aback if you haven't yet explained this custom to him. Your father can then mention the expected amount. By this time, he will be so accustomed to buying you gifts and providing that he won't protest much.

Ask your parents to see the ring before he proposes. They will peruse it to make sure it's worthy of their daughter's lifelong commitment. They can take some time to thoughtfully assess the ring's quality and suitability. After some deliberation they will approve or disapprove depending on this appraisal.

This interaction will mostly be for show. If your simp makes it into the courtship net, he has already taken the bait to win your affections. That said, the anticipation of waiting for your parent's approval will keep him on his toes. This moment, although somewhat ceremonial, serves to ensuring he remains attentive and committed as the relationship progresses to this important milestone.

CHAPTER FIFTY-FOUR

TEASE BUT DON'T PLEASE

Your simp may be so overcome with your beauty that he will barely keep his hands off you. However, unlike the average girl, TWG are prepared to keep his octopus arms at bay.

Though you have indulged in some suggestive and borderline sexy conversations, you wisely curtailed his attempts to coerce you into webcamming.

You relied on your conservative culture and upbringing as your "get out of jail card" when he whined about test driving the car before buying as he does with American women.

When you meet in person, bring your parents or older brother to chaperone your interactions and prevent any hanky panky that could bring dishonor on the family (Even if this is BS, play it up). That said, DO allow him to steal a brief kiss and cop a feel before gently removing his hands as your watchdogs return from their bathroom break. Your Academy award winning performance will let your simp know that you find him just as attractive as he finds you.

Slowly lower your gaze to his lips. Linger for a long second. Then raise you gaze to meet his eyes. This will create an insatiable hunger in loins to possess you.

Yet, it is a meal that can only be enjoyed within the sanctity of marriage. Once he gets the ring on your finger, you will give in to passions long denied. As you hold hands and tap your thumb rhythmically space between his thumb and forefinger, the pulsations will conjure images of your bodies becoming one. This simple, suggestive touch will drive him mad to have you!

CHAPTER FIFTY-FIVE

SAYING YES

Your simp proposes, and you accept. Amidst the joyous cheers of your friends and family, you embrace, excited for the impending nuptials. However, this moment is not the final destination. Despite passing all your tests, there's a chance he may hesitate to walk down the aisle.

He might mistakenly believe that being engaged entitles him to pre-game conjugal visits, or he may have proposed out of fear of losing you, seeking to buy time and appease you.

At this stage, you and your family should embark on a campaign to urge your simp to pursue the fiancée visa. If he's American, he should initiate the process by filing a petition for an alien fiancée, using form 1-129F. This initial step sets the groundwork for obtaining the K-1 fiancee visa.

Upon entering the US on the K-1 visa, you must marry within 90 days. Once married within this timeframe, you gain access to the coveted "Holy Grail" - the Green Card.

Please note that this is not intended as legal advice. It's advisable to seek guidance from a specialized attorney for the most accurate and up-to-date information regarding your situation.

CHAPTER FIFTY-SIX
THE CULTURAL BARRIER

If your simp checks most of your boxes and your intention is to stay wedded for the long haul, you might still be concerned because of the cultural and linguistic differences.

The cultural barrier between you and your intended, instead of being an obstacle, provides unique advantages. The demands that would outrage him if it came out of an American woman's mouth, land differently when his foreign bride says it. Spoken in your adorable native accent, what you say is excused as a part of your upbringing.

Imagine this: You, the spitfire foreign bride, declare to your American beau, "Tom! We must marry in three months or we cannot be together!" In your thick, pidgin English accent, this statement sounds less like an ultimatum and more like an courtship ritual that is consistent with your community traditions.

Being a foreign bride allows for what can be termed "plausible deniability." Cultural differences might lead to misunderstandings, but they also provide an excuse to overlook or forgive certain behaviors. It's easier for your partner to attribute any unusual demands or behaviors to cultural differences rather than personal flaws or incompatibility. Poor Tom is left wondering if agreeing to jump into marriage with a gal he barely knows is a third world custom or if he's just unwittingly agreed to star in a rom-com full of misunderstandings.

In America, he would dump a girl who wouldn't put out by the third date; but on your exotic shores he is ready to put a ring on it with barely more than a kiss to seal the deal!

In essence, your cultural and linguistic uniqueness adds a layer of intrigue *and* forgiveness in the relationship. Did you just insult his mother, or is that comment how people compliment each other in your language?

He won't be able to tell the difference. By this time, he will be so besotted with you, it won't matter.

CHAPTER FIFTY-SEVEN
WEDDED BLISS

It is important to retain the façade of the traditional, submissive wife who adores the ground her husband walks on. He must feel like he won the lottery when he found you. You are the complete package and the polar opposite of the entitled thots back home. Rest assured he will parade you in front of the grown up popular jocks and cheerleaders who never noticed nor appreciated him back home.

As a married woman, you give him access to your body long denied. It will be the best sex he has ever had. Maybe it's the *only* sex he's ever had. Why will he love it so much? Because he had to earn it. Men only appreciate what they have to work for. If it's free, it's trash; that's why he doesn't value the American chicks who put out by the third date back home!

Be enthusiastic to receive him, no matter how old and ugly he is. However, never be too available. Now that he has had a taste of your supple skin, snatch it away on occasion, like Lucy with a football. There will be some days that you will have a stomachache, or your period, or a headache. He will long for you even more with a pinch of scarcity.

Men are simple. Be their second mommy, to keep them satisfied. Cook and clean so that he returns to a tidy home and dinner hot from the oven after work. Be a sounding board for their problems as they relax in their easy chair after dinner.

Make him feel good. He will remember how you make him feel and seek you again and again, for another hit of your feminine narcotic. Let him bask in the high of your feminine power. Then remove it from under his nose when he least expects it, so that your absence feels like torture. Give him another bump to soothe his withdrawal.

You have made him a lifelong addict!

CHAPTER FIFTY-EIGHT
THE SQUIRREL

Given that your legal status may not permit you to work when you first arrive in your new country, you'll likely find yourself in the role of a stay-at-home wife (and you've already spelled out that you will be a housewife). However, it's important to have access to funds for groceries and managing household expenses. Considering your husband's history of sending gifts and money during your courtship, it's reasonable to expect that he won't object to providing you with a regular allowance for these necessities.

Though unlikely thanks to your thorough vetting process, there is always a chance that once you are both settled onto American soil, he may revert to his incel/dusty ways. You must prepare for this possibility.

From your allowance money, you will skim 10% off the top and hide it somewhere in the home or consider renting a safety deposit box. Store it where he will never find it.

You will need a secret stash in case things go south. After all, there was a reason he, unlike his compadres, was unable to settle down in his prime, when he a headful of hair and optimal muscle mass. His singleness was caused by being socially or physically maladjusted in some way.

Be aware that although you did your best to vet him before marriage, there may be some skeletons in the closet that came tumbling out. Only after cohabitating with him 24/7 will you truly know who he is at his core. Messy or OCD, Mama's boy or sissy—you will find out once the honeymoon period is over.

As you settle into married life in your new country, you might start noticing your husband's peculiarities becoming more pronounced. It's possible that, over time, these quirks might even escalate--challenging your resolve to stand by his side.

To prepare for any unforeseen circumstances, think of yourself as a prudent squirrel gearing up for winter. It's wise to start discreetly saving - a financial safety net that's just for you. This advice isn't just for those in new countries; it resonates with our American audience too. Remember the old wisdom of grandmothers stashing away emergency funds in their mattresses? That hidden reserve can provide a reassuring sense of security as you navigate family life.

We suggest aiming to save at least $5,000.00. This amount can serve as a safety cushion, offering you the flexibility and means to make a swift exit if the situation ever demands it.

CHAPTER FIFTY-NINE
KEEP HIM DREADED

While you offer the charm and excitement of your feminine presence, he must never feel completely secure that he has you. The fact that you are out of his league by being younger, fitter and prettier than him will add one dimension of dread. The other layer you will supply by switching up your routine every so often to keep him guessing.

Being unpredictable is something men say they hate but secretly love. They like not knowing what will happen next. Your mystery is what makes you uniquely a woman.

Cultivating "dread game" ensures that your husband never feels 100% secure and thwarts the complacency that afflicts many marriages.

Being unpredictable doesn't always mean being unreliable. You should aim to be consistently inconsistent. This can be achieved simply as changing your clothing style, wearing new lipstick, or taking up a new hobby. It's about creating a sense of mystery and keeping him in a state of curiosity about you.

Return home late on rare occasions. Resist the urge to answer his texts immediately. Here and there, wait an hour or so before responding.

Remember, your uniqueness as a woman is not just about your youth and beauty but also in your ability to keep him guessing. Your feminine mystique is as important an asset as your looks and an integral facet of your sex appeal.

CHAPTER SIXTY

KEEP HIM OBSESSED

Though we warned you about future fakers and love bombers, we are not opposed to using kinder and gentler versions of these tactics to domesticate our simp.

You are the purveyor of the fantasy. He has already been exposed to these concepts by RP podcasters and Passport Bros who clutch their pearls about the degenerate state of American women. Agree and amplify their perceptions about Western women.

Do not disappoint them. Sell him on the fantasy that he desperately wants to be true: that somewhere, in a secluded island far, far, away, is a paradise of traditional, conservative, sex-positive (but chaste) virgins waiting for their American savior to pluck them (and fuck them) out of their humble circumstances.

You will make him feel like he has entered Heaven on Earth.

Why, yes, you will happily fold his laundry and cook him delicious meals from scratch. You will wait for him by the door with your negligee on, ready, willing and able to satisfy his desires (that you will enthusiastically match) any time of the day. Your body will not change after you give him babies and you will do whatever it takes to get back into the same shape as the woman that first attracted him. You will give him "the world".

Once married, weave in elements of his fantasy, but do not serve it all it once, and do not serve it every day. A man thinks that when he gets what he wants, he will be happy. When in fact, it is not the *getting*, but the act of PURSUING that makes him feel alive.

CHAPTER SIXTY-ONE

BE SELFISH

Women are conditioned to be selfless. We are programmed to act in the best interest of our children, our husbands, and our community.

This selflessness, taken to the extreme, will result in our destruction.

Think about this—how many women die at the hands of their spouses? Did you know that one of the leading causes of death of pregnant women is murder by her romantic partner?

This is the sobering reality of women who choose men emotionally, rather than logically.

Once a woman is emotionally invested, it is difficult to extricate herself from her relationship, even if it is toxic. Especially if it is toxic! The Stockholm syndrome is real. A dysfunctional dynamic, in which the victim of the abuse seeks validation from her abuser, can keep a woman trapped in a mental and physical prison for a lifetime.

Men, on the other hand, rarely "love" to their own destruction. They are much more conditioned to act in their own self-interest. This is why men more often leave marriages and children simply for being "unhappy".

Whereas a woman, even if she is being neglected, taken for granted, cheated on, or abused, tends to tolerate these hardships much longer than a man will. She feels a sense of obligation to her partner and will do everything in her power to make it work. Only when she has reached her breaking point does an invested woman walk away.

When she does walk away, the pain will be intense, but after a mourning period, the feeling will fade. Women are blessed with amnesia once the relationship is dead and buried. It will be like he never existed.

(This is the polar opposite of how men process breakups. They will initially feel overjoyed and free. Often they will jump into new relationships right away. Months later they will be overcome with grief and contact their exes for forgiveness and beg to be taken back. More on this in book 2.)

However, we want you to skip this entire sordid episode. Better to educate yourself than to waste your time enmeshed with a dusty emotionally and financially.

This is where you will take a page from men's game. Rather than embroider your life to placate a man, or society, or your friends, you will put yourself first. Decide what you want, execute your personal blueprint. Remember, you are the VIP of your life!

CHAPTER SIXTY-TWO
UNCONDITIONAL LOVE

Unconditional love between a man and a woman is a fairy tale. The kind of love that remains steadfast regardless of age, weight, income, and health exists only between a mother and her children.

There are women who spend their entire lives chasing the dragon. They're deceived into believing if they search tirelessly, sacrifice and compromise their standards, that they will find a man who loves them unconditionally.

This is a fool's errand that saps women of their vitality in their most precious years. A woman would be better served to take her focus off the *promise* to be loved and cherished forever and set her sights on tangible rewards instead.

Talk is cheap. Declarations of love don't pay the bills. Non-legally binding vows to provide and protect are as enforceable as the imaginary paper they're drawn upon.

Many women have been promised the moon and the stars, only to be left with an empty bag. Consider the women in your life who built up and supported their dusty husbands, only to be traded in for a newer model when they reached the pinnacle of his professional success. Imagine how different her outcome would have been had she allowed her ex to work hard and simp for her. Even in the event of a divorce she would be financially secure from the savings she socked away while he climbed up the professional ladder.

Demolish your preconceived ideas unconditional love in the hereafter and focus on the tangible realities in the here and now. True love can only be attested to by provision and support.

CHAPTER SIXTY-THREE
STACEY WINS

The manosphere and pickmeisha have one thing in common—their ire that no matter what sins she has committed -- Stacey wins. Women that are bubbly, fun, and extroverted will never have any trouble finding a husband. And not just any man—she will effortlessly secure a high value mate, at any age.

Redpillers with sour grapes that Stacey has the gall to find happiness and not be "held accountable" for rejecting incels will label the man she marries as a "Beta". After all, a true Alpha with hundreds of options would never submit to marriage with a used up former party girl.

However, it is not men who defines what an Alpha versus a Beta is. Women define the hierarchy of men. An Alpha *is* a simp.

A man who is promiscuous and will not commit is a **liability** to a woman. The playboy will put her health at risk of STD's. He will likely abandon the children she bears.

Hitching one's wagon to a broke playboy is akin to swallowing a slow releasing poison. Pickmeisha's children will suffer the consequences of her poor choices, as they lack leadership and provision from their deadbeat dads.

A woman with a modicum of sense will only marry a playboy if there is an incentive. The American woman may take the risk if he is wealthy enough and pop out a kid to guarantee an allowance for the next 18 years. The richer and older he is (with pre-existing health conditions), the better! See Elon Musk and Mick Jagger.

TWG will marry any man with a pulse as long as he gives her access to a green card and a wallet. She is playing the long game.

However, the vast majority of men are not in the top 1% of income producers. Only 1.5% of Americans make over $300k per year, a figure now considered to reflect the upper middle class! Therefore, there is little incentive for a woman to compromise her health and her uterus to submit to the whims of a suburban lower middle class so-called Alpha.

Wise women reject the RP definition of an "Alpha". The RP definition of an Alpha provides no value. For us, a true Alpha provides, protects and creates a secure environment for his wife and their children to survive.

A "body count" is no impediment to Stacey's success in securing an Alpha husband. If a simp's wooden soldier stands at attention when she walks into a room, her personal history is irrelevant. His attraction will override his ideology.

This can actually be frustrating to the "good girl" Pickmeisha who has played by the rules, devoutly attends church, and dresses modestly. She has dedicated her entire life in hopes of being chosen as a trad wife, only to watch the reformed sorority sister snatch the most eligible bachelors a millisecond after she has repented for her girls-gone-wild ways!

We exaggerate here for emphasis, as the majority of women (98%) do not have OF accounts, nor have they ever appeared in porn, or worked as a prostitute. However, the point stands, that if you satisfy men's sexual niches and do not succumb to shaming tactics from your rivals meant to keep you sick, poor and isolated—you will come out on top.

These spinsters in training have been misled to believe that wearing makeup, keeping fit, and flirting are jezebel tactics. Good men should choose them because of their virtue, cooking skills and low maintenance demands. Imagine their dismay when the opposite is shown to be true, and they are invisible to the single men in their community.

The discourse on social media reflects this dilemma. So-called religious men express their frustration at the scarcity of religious women at worship services. "I can't find any Christian girls at church!" they claim. "All of the women are taken!"

In reality, women outnumber men in church. In some denominations, the gender ratio can be as high as 60-65% women to 35-40% men. Some localized studies suggest that the ratio of single women to single men can be as high as 2:1!

Clearly, it is false that there are no single religious women for single religious men to choose from. The men remain single because the outgoing, fun and attractive women have already been taken. The leftover women are typically plain, overweight, and shy. To them, these unattractive women are non-entities! Unless a reformed hoe with a heart of gold walks into the pews seeking absolution, it's likely that the religious male will stay single and redirect his simping behaviors toward a charismatic spiritual leader or reinvent himself as a chaste defender of the faith, like St. Paul.

Therefore, we advise women to ignore the advice to play small. If you are of a religious bent, like our example above, we suggest you get out of your comfort zone. Visit the cosmetics aisle and request a natural-looking makeover. Because you are used to looking like a pilgrim fresh off the Mayflower, you might feel like a red district harlot when you see your rosy cheeks and dusky eyelashes in the mirror. Resist the urge to rub it off. Next, go upstairs to the clothing section of the department store. Ask one of the shopgirls to help you pick out fashionable but tasteful outfits. Even if you aren't at your ideal weight, form fitting dresses will flatter your figure more than the potato sacks in your closet.

Perhaps one of the biggest challenges to overcome is excessive shyness. A reserved demeanor can be mysterious and can spark a man's curiosity. The problem arises when shyness veers into closed off body language and socially awkward affects, which will make you unapproachable.

To chip away at this cumbersome trait we suggest getting a part time job that requires social interaction. A job as a barista at a coffee shop in an affluent neighborhood will allow you to practice smiling and making eye contact with well-to-do customers. Developing the art of conservation may not come naturally to you, but with practice, you will feel more confident in your skin, which is magnetic.

Another strategy to overcome shyness is to do volunteer work. Volunteering will allow you to mingle without the sweaty palms and awkward silences of dating. Start out by finding a cause that you're passionate about and get involved with their non-profit advocacy. You can even seek ones out that are male dominated such as Habitat for Humanity. Volunteering for galas in ritzy neighborhoods, will guarantee a "meet cute" with a Bruce Wayne or two. It's a win-win-win: you help out a great cause, watch rich men trying to outbid each other for who can donate the most, and network for career and romantic prospects.

Once you have maximized your looks and improved your approachability, your dating results will improve. These exercises will open doors to meaningful connections, whatever your environment is.

Rather than hate Stacey because she always lands on her feet, learn from her. Bring your "A" game. Cultivate your mystery. Maximize your looks. Smell good. Flirt. Have a problem only he can solve. Be fun. Never be 100% predictable.

Your dance card will be full. Voila! You will have successfully tamed the lone wolves into a loyal puppies, eagerly wagging their tails at the mere sight of you.

Men desire to simp. They crave it. Despite any protestations to the contrary, they will find their greatest happiness when they embrace their natural inclination to submit to their lady love.

Thanks to your personal brew of intermittent attention, in-person warmth and affection, and the occasional treat, the once self-sufficient Mr. Independent has morphed into a simp whose life goal is to make you happy.

Ladies, if you can't beat 'em, join em. Stop being a wall flower and start your glow up!

CHAPTER SIXTY-FOUR

IS IT WORTH IT?

We're presenting this chapter as we near the conclusion of this book to serve as a poignant reminder of the purpose behind your journey. At this juncture, some of you may find yourselves grappling with doubts, questioning whether you possess the resilience required to navigate the path to finding Mr. Right. It's natural to feel disheartened, especially if you've dedicated significant portions of your life to the service of unappreciative partners and family.

But amidst these feelings of frustration and disillusionment, do not to succumb to bitterness. Instead, channel your emotions into a drive for self-improvement. Rather than asking the Creator why you weren't born as a natural "Stacey," who seemingly glides through life with suitors eating out of her hand, emulate her.

Relish the opportunity to elevate yourself, not through comparison, but through radical introspection. Recognize that your journey is uniquely yours.

Every simp setback presents an opportunity to refine your roster. ALL MEN ARE SIMPS; what one won't do, another will. By reframing your experiences, you empower yourself to transcend the limitations imposed by scarcity minded relatives and friends who urge you to settle for the next dusty who crosses your path.

Keep your "why" at the forefront of your mind. You're undertaking this journey for the opportunity to attain a better life, to break free from the cycles of poverty and abuse, and to forge a lasting legacy for yourself and your children.

CHAPTER SIXTY-FIVE
IN SUM, GET YOU SOME

We hope you have enjoyed our introduction to the art of the finesse. These guidelines will equip you with a basic understanding on how to bait the hook and catch your simp. As you apply these principles, you're setting the stage for significant and positive changes in your life. Look forward to Part Two, where we will delve deeper into advanced strategies and techniques.

In the meantime, we suggest reading these classics as you prepare yourself for this journey.

"How to Win Friends and Influence People" by Dale Carnegie

"The Game of Life and How to Win It" by Florence Scoville Shinn

While it might seem like we're emphasizing the obvious, we are well aware that readers like to skip to the last chapter. Tuck these thoughts away and let them guide you as you happily date.

1. Never fall in love. Grow in love.
2. Stay detached.
3. Be his (not quite attainable) dream girl.
4. Be Playful.
5. Stick to your boundaries.
6. View relationships as a business.
7. Until he invests in you financially, it's all talk.
8. All love is conditional love.
9. Use cultural and linguistic differences to your advantage.
10. Learn from Stacey.

11. Seal the deal.
12. Know when to walk away…and know when to run.